W9-BVF-166

Table of Contents

Comprehension and Context 3
Comprehension: Word Origins 4
Fact or Opinion? 5
Main Idea 6
Using the Dictionary 7
Writing a Summary 8, 9
Comprehension Crossword 10
Using Prior Knowledge: Music 11
Main Idea: Where Did Songs
    Come From? 12
Comprehension: Facts About
    Folk Music 13
Recalling Details: "Little Tommy Tucker" 14
Comprehension: Jazz Notes 15
Recalling Details: Woodwinds 16
Comprehension: Harp Happenings . . . 17
Comprehension: Brass Shows Class . . . 18
Comprehension: Violins 19
Review **20**
Using Prior Knowledge: Farm Animals . 21
Sequencing: "Little Bo-Peep" 22
Comprehension: All About Sheep 23
Recalling Details: "Little Boy Blue" 24
Comprehension: Pigs Are Particular . . 25
Context Clues: No Kidding About
    Goats 26
Comprehension: Cows Are
    Complicated 27
Context Clues: Dairy Cows 28
Comprehension: Chickens 29
Review **30, 31**
Using Prior Knowledge: Books 32
Context Clues: Remember Who
    You Are 33
Comprehension: Books and
    More Books! 34
Comprehension: Help for
    the Homeless 35
Fact or Opinion? 36

Context Clues: Kids' Books Are
    Big Business 37
Review **38**
Using Prior Knowledge: Cooking 39
Following Directions: Chunky Tomato
    and Green Onion Sauce 40
Comprehension: Cooking With Care . . . 41
Sequencing: Chocolate Chunk Cookies . . 42
Comprehension: Eating High-Fiber Foods . 43
Main Idea: New Corn 44
Comprehension: The French
    Eat Differently 45
Comprehension: Chinese Cabbage 46
Review **47**
Using Prior Knowledge: Greek
    and Roman Mythology 48
Comprehension: Roman Legends 49
Comprehension: Apollo and Phaethon . . . 50
Context Clues: Mighty Hercules 51
Comprehension: Ceres and Venus 52
Comprehension: Proserpine and Pluto 53
Comprehension: Orpheus Saves the Day . 54
Recalling Details: Centaurs
    and Minotaurs 55
Review **56, 57**
Using Prior Knowledge: Art 58
Main Idea: Creating Art 59
Comprehension: Leonardo da Vinci 60
Context Clues: Leonardo da Vinci 61
Comprehension: Michelangelo 62
Recalling Details: Michelangelo Puzzler . . . 63
Comprehension: Rembrandt 64
Recalling Details: Rembrandt Puzzler 65
Comprehension: More About Rembrandt . 66
Review **67**
Using Prior Knowledge: Stamp Collecting . 68
Fact or Opinion? 69
Comprehension: More About Stamp
Collecting 70

Table of Contents

Recalling Details: Philately
Abbreviations 71
Comprehension: Faces on Stamps . . . 72
Recalling Details: Postage
Stamp Puzzler 73
Comprehension: Valuable Stamps 74
Fact or Opinion? 75
Comprehension: Stamp Value 76
Review **77**
Using Prior Knowledge: Writing 78
Comprehension: Calling Young Poets
and Writers! 79
Comprehension: Poems for
Kids of All Ages 80
Comprehension: *Highlights
for Children* 81
Sequencing: Studying the Market 82
Comprehension: "The Trains" 83
Comprehension/Sequencing:
Limericks 84
Review **85**
Using Prior Knowledge: Big Cats 86
Comprehension: Jaguars 87
Comprehension: Leopards 88
Comprehension: Lynxes 89
Comprehension: Pumas 90
Comprehension: Cheetahs 91
Comprehension: Tigers 92
Comprehension: Lions 93
Recalling Details: Big Cats 94
Review **95**
Using Prior Knowledge: Famous Ships . 96
Comprehension: The *Constitution* 97
Comprehension: The *Santa Maria,
Niña* and *Pinta* 98
Comprehension: The *Lusitania* 99
Comprehension: The *Titanic* 100
Venn Diagram: The *Lusitania*
and *Titanic* 101

Comprehension: The *Monitor*
and the *Virginia* 102
Review **103**
Cumulative Review **104–106**
Glossary 107
Answer Key 108–125
Teaching Suggestions 126–128

Name: Lauren

Comprehension and Context

Comprehension is understanding what is seen, heard or read.

Context is the rest of the words in a sentence or the sentences before or after a word. Context can help with comprehension.

Context clues help you figure out the meaning of a word by relating it to other words in the sentence.

Directions: Use the context clues in the sentences to find the meanings of the bold words.

1. Jane was a **wizard** at games. She mastered them in no time and seldom lost.

   ☐ evil magician   ☒ gifted person   ☐ average player

2. The holiday was so special that she was sure she'd never forget it. The memory would be **imprinted** forever on her mind.

   ☐ found   ☐ weighed   ☒ fixed

3. "John will believe anything anyone tells him," his teacher said. "He's a very **impressionable** young man."

   ☒ easily influenced   ☐ unhappy   ☐ unintelligent

4. "Do you really think it's **prudent** to spend all your money on clothes?" his mother asked crossly.

   ☐ foolish   ☒ wise   ☐ funny

5. "Your plan has **merit**," Elizabeth's father said. "Let me give it some thought."

   ☒ value   ☐ awards   ☐ kindness

6. John was very **gregarious** and loved being around people.

   ☐ shy   ☒ outgoing   ☐ unfriendly

© 1999 American Education Publishing Co.

Name: Lauren

Comprehension: Word Origins

Did you ever wonder why we call our mid-day meal "lunch"? Or where the name "Abraham" came from? Or why one of our lovely eastern states is called "Vermont"?

These and other words have a history. The study of where words came from and how they began is called **etymology** (ett-a-mol-o-gee).

The word **lunch** comes from the Spanish word **longja**, which means "a slice of ham." Long ago, Spanish people ate a slice of ham for their mid-day meal. Eventually, what they ate became the word for the meal itself. Still later, it came to be pronounced "lunch" in English.

Abraham also has an interesting history. Originally, it came from the Hebrew word **avarahem**. Abraham means "father of many."

City and state names are often based on the names of Native American tribes or describe the geography of the area. **Vermont** is actually made from two French words. **Vert** is French for "green." **Mont** is French for "mountain."

Directions: Answer these questions about word origins.

1. What is the study of the history and origin of words? _Etymology_

2. From which language did the word **lunch** come? _Spanish_

3. What is the French word for "green"? _Vert_

4. **Vermont** comes from two words of what language?

☐ Spanish   ☐ English   ☒ French

5. Which is not correct about the origin of names of cities and states?

☒ They describe geography.

☒ They name Native American tribes.

☒ They are mostly French in origin.

Name: Lauren

Fact or Opinion?

A **fact** is information that can be proven true. An **opinion** is information that tells how someone feels or what he/she thinks about something or someone.

Directions: Read the paragraph below. Then, in the corresponding numbered blanks, write whether each numbered sentence is a fact or an opinion.

(1) What to do about homeless people has become an important issue in most big cities. (2) Some people believe federal money should be spent to provide housing. (3) Others think these people should somehow find a way to take care of themselves. (4) Among those raising money for the homeless are bookstores. (5) In Los Angeles, for example, a group called "Booksellers and Writers Against Homelessness" held a series of fund-raisers for homeless people. (6) What a wonderful thing for these people to do! (7) The *Los Angeles Daily News* also helped bring public attention to the homeless through a front-page article. (8) The article told about a shelter for homeless women in the San Fernando Valley that was in desperate need of funds. (9) As a result of the article, hundreds of people sent donations to the shelter. (10) Americans are very generous!

1. Fact
2. Opinion
3. Opinion
4. Fact
5. Fact

A+

6. Opinion
7. Fact
8. Fact
9. Fact
10. Opinion

Name: Lauren

Main Idea

The **main idea** is the most important idea, or main point, in a sentence, paragraph or story.

Directions: Read the paragraphs below. For each paragraph, underline the sentence that tells the main idea.

Sometimes people think they have to choose between exercise and fun. For many people, it is more fun to watch television than to run 5 miles. Yet, if you don't exercise, your body gets soft and out of shape. You move more slowly. You may even think more slowly. But why do something that isn't fun? Well, there are many ways to exercise and have fun.

One family solved the exercise problem by using their TV. They hooked up the television to an electric generator. The generator was operated by an exercise bike. Anyone who wanted to watch TV had to ride the bike. The room with their television in it must have been quite a sight!

Think of the times when you are just "hanging out" with your friends. You go outside and jump rope, play ball, run races, and so on. Soon you are all laughing and having a good time. Many group activities can provide you with exercise and be fun, too.

Maybe there aren't enough kids around after school for group games. Perhaps you are by yourself. Then what? You can get plenty of exercise just by walking, biking or even dancing. In the morning, walk the long way to the bus. Ride your bike to and from school. Practice the newest dance by yourself. Before you know it, you will be the fittest dancer of all your friends!

Directions: Write other ideas you have for combining fun and exercise below.

I think that jogging could be a very good exercise. Anthor thing you can do is practice favorite sport. Every day you can do some exercise like jump roping. I think every day you should atleast do a few pushups or curl-ups. You can alˢᵒ pick a sport to play that is a great exercise!!

Grade- B+

Name: Lauren

Using the Dictionary

Guide words are the words that appear at the top of dictionary pages. They show the first and last words on each page.

Directions: Read the guide words on each dictionary page below. Then look around for objects whose names come between the guide words. Write the names of the objects, and then number them in alphabetical order.

babble	bowl	buzz
	bear	ɾ

magic		myself

cabin		cycle

pea		puzzle

dairy		dwarf

scar		sword

feast		future

tack		truth

Name: _____

Writing a Summary

A **summary** is a short description of what a selection or book is about.

Directions: Read the following selection and the example summary.

Fads of the 1950s

A fad is a practice or an object that becomes very popular for a period of time. Recent popular fads include yo-yos and Beanie Babies®. In the 1950s, there were many different fads, including coonskin caps, hula hoops and 3-D movies.

Coonskin caps were made popular by the weekly television show about Davy Crockett, which began in December of 1954. Not only did Davy's hat itself become popular but anything with Davy Crockett on it was in hot demand.

Also popular were hula hoops. They were produced by the Wham-O company in 1958. The company had seen similar toys in Australia. Hula hoops were priced at $1.98, and over 30 million hoops were sold within 6 months.

Another fad was the 3-D movie. When television sets began to appear in every American home, the movie industry began to suffer financially. Movie companies rushed to produce 3-D movies, and movie-goers once more flocked to theaters. The first 3-D movie was shown in Los Angeles on November 26, 1952. People loved the special Polaroid® glasses and scenes in the movie that seemed to jump out at them. As with the hula hoop and Davy Crockett, people soon tired of 3-D movies, and they became old news as they were replaced by new fads.

Summary

Over the years, many fads have become popular with the American public. During the 1950s, three popular fads were the hula hoop, Davy Crockett and 3-D movies. Davy Crockett's coonskin cap became a fad with the beginning of the weekly television show. Hula hoops were sold by the millions, and 3-D movies were enjoyed by people everywhere. However, like all fads, interest in these items soon died out.

Name: Lauren

Writing a Summary

Directions: Read the following selection. Using page 8 as a guide, write a summary of the selection.

Man's First Flights

In the first few years of the 20th century, the majority of people strongly believed that man could not and would not ever be able to fly. There were a few daring individuals who worked to prove the public wrong.

On December 8, 1903, Samuel Langley attempted to fly his version of an airplane from the roof of a houseboat on the Potomac River. Langley happened to be the secretary of the Smithsonian Institution, so his flight was covered not only by news reporters but also by government officials. Unfortunately, his trip met with sudden disaster when his aircraft did a nose dive into the river.

Nine days later, brothers Orville and Wilbur Wright attempted a flight. They had assembled their aircraft at their home in Dayton, Ohio, and shipped it to Kitty Hawk, North Carolina. On December 17, the Wright brothers made several flights, the longest one lasting an incredible 59 seconds. Since the Wright brothers had kept their flight attempts secret, their miraculous flight was only reported by two newspapers in the United States.

At first people in the 20th century said man could not fly. Though on December, 1903 they were proved wrong. Samuel Langley Attemted to try flg his version of a plane. Though Langley's idea turned in to a disaster, his plane crashed. Nine days after brothors Orville and Wilbur Wright attemptted a flight. They made several flights, their longest time was 59 secounds. The Wright Kept their flight a secret so only 2 newspapers reported the flight.

Grade - 100%

9

Comprehension Crossword

Directions: Use the clues from the box to complete the crossword puzzle.

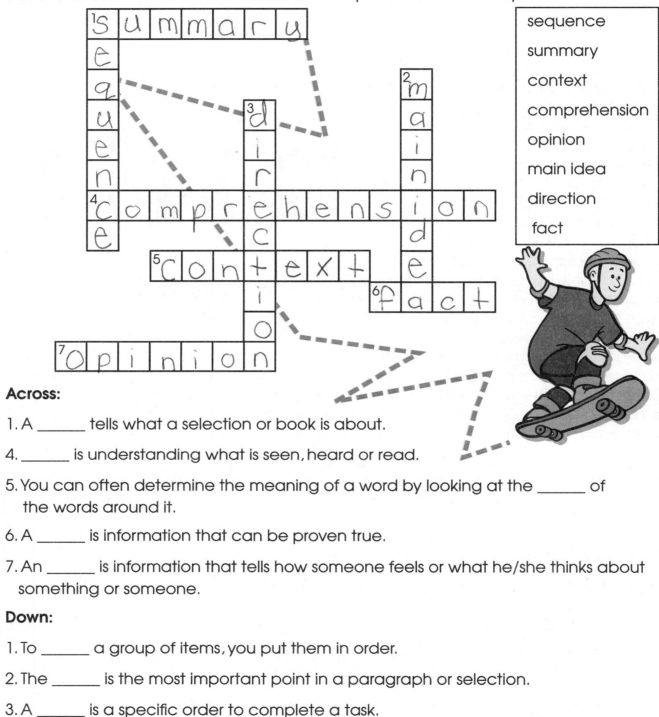

sequence
summary
context
comprehension
opinion
main idea
direction
fact

Across:

1. A _____ tells what a selection or book is about.

4. _____ is understanding what is seen, heard or read.

5. You can often determine the meaning of a word by looking at the _____ of the words around it.

6. A _____ is information that can be proven true.

7. An _____ is information that tells how someone feels or what he/she thinks about something or someone.

Down:

1. To _____ a group of items, you put them in order.

2. The _____ is the most important point in a paragraph or selection.

3. A _____ is a specific order to complete a task.

Name: Lauren

Using Prior Knowledge: Music

Using **prior knowledge** means being able to use what one already knows to find an answer or get information.

Directions: Before reading about music in the following section, answer these questions.

1. In your opinion, why is music important to people?

I think music is imortent to because music can express your feelings. Music can make you feel good

2. Name as many styles of music as you can.

Alto, Soprano, rock, country, blues, pop, Latin, jazz, Orchestra, band,

3. What is your favorite type of music? Why?

I like pop because alot of my favorite songs are pop. I also like pop because you can sing a slow song or dance song,

4. If you could choose a musical instrument to play, what would it be? Why?

If I could choose an instrument to play it claranet. I would play clarenet because I love the sound of it it can go low or high

5. Name a famous musician and describe what you know about him/her.

A famouse musician that I have heard of is Loey Amstrong. I heard that he was a great trumpet player. I know that he was one of the best musicians in the world

11

Main Idea: Where Did Songs Come From?

Historians say the earliest music was probably connected to religion. Long ago, people believed the world was controlled by a variety of gods. Singing was among the first things humans did to show respect to the gods.

Singing is still an important part of most religions. Buddhists (bood-ists), Christians and Jews all use chants and/or songs in their religious ceremonies. If you have ever sung a song—religious or otherwise—you know that singing is fun. The feeling of joy that comes from singing must also have made ancient people feel happy.

Another time people sang was when they worked. Egyptian slaves sang as they carried the heavy stones to build the pyramids. Soldiers sang as they marched into battle. Farmers sang one song as they planted and another when they harvested. Singing made the work less burdensome. People used the tunes to pace themselves. Sometimes they followed instructions through songs. For example, "Yo-oh, heave ho!/Yo-oh, heave ho!" was sung when sailors pulled on a ship's ropes to lift the sails. **Heave** means "to lift," and that is what they did as they sang the song. The song helped sailors work together and pull at the same time. This made the task easier.

Directions: Answer these questions about music.

1. Circle the main idea:

OOPS! Singing is fun, and that is why early people liked it so much.

Singing began as a way to show respect to the gods and is still an important part of most religious ceremonies.

Traditionally, singing has been important as a part of religious ceremonies and as inspiration to workers.

2. Besides religious ceremonies, what other activity fostered singing? _It helped people work, like sailors and Egyptions_

3. When did farmers sing two different songs? _When the sailors pulled the sails_

4. How did singing "Yo-oh, heave ho!" help sailors work? _It helped the sailors work together and pull at the same time._

Name: Lauren

Comprehension: Facts About Folk Music

Folk music literally means music "of the folks," and it belongs to everyone. The names of the musicians who composed most folk music have long been forgotten. Even so, folk music has remained popular because it tells about the lives of people. Usually, the tune is simple, and even though folk songs often have many verses, the words are easy to remember. Do you know the words to "She'll Be Comin' 'Round the Mountain"?

Although no one ever says who "she" is, the verses tell you that she will be "riding six white horses" and that "we'll go out to greet her." The song also describes what will be eaten when she comes (chicken and dumplings) and what those singing will be wearing (red pajamas).

"Clementine" is a song that came out of the California gold rush in the mid-1800s. It tells the story of a woman who was "lost and gone forever" when she was killed. ("In a cavern, in a canyon, excavating for a mine/Met a miner '49er and his daughter, Clementine.")

Another famous folk song is "Swing Low, Sweet Chariot." This song was sung by slaves in the United States and today is sung by people of all races. The words "Swing low, sweet chariot, coming for to carry me home . . ." describe the soul being united with God after death. Like other folk songs that sprang from slaves, "Swing Low, Sweet Chariot" is simple, moving and powerful.

Directions: Answer these questions about folk music.

1. What is the purpose of folk music? _The purpose of folk music is to tell about peoples lives_

2. What food is sung about in "She'll Be Comin' 'Round the Mountain"? _In the it says she will eat chicken and dumplings_

3. Where did Clementine live?

☐ Florida   ☐ Mississippi   ☑ California

4. Where in the United States do you think "Swing Low, Sweet Chariot" was first sung?

☐ the North   ☐ the West   ☑ the South

Name: _____

Recalling Details: "Little Tommy Tucker"

Recalling details means to be able to pick out and remember the who, what, when, where, why and how of what is being read.

Little Tommy Tucker

Sings for his supper.

What shall he eat?

Brown bread and butter.

How shall he cut it

Without any knife?

How shall he marry

Without any wife?

Directions: Answer these questions about "Little Tommy Tucker."

1. What does Tommy have to do to get his supper? _For supper Tommy has to sing._

2. What does he eat for supper? _He eats brown bread and butter for supper._

3. What two things does Tommy not have? _Tommy sings for both an knife and a wife._

Name: _____

Comprehension: Jazz Notes

Jazz, which began in the southern United States, became popular in the late 1800s. Like some folk songs, jazz was the music made by African American people. It was the music of former slaves.

The rhythm and the beat of early jazz reflected the roots of black Americans in Africa. Many early jazz musicians could not read music. They sometimes made up their music as they went along on their clarinets, trumpets and other instruments. This "on-the-spot composing" is called "improvising." Modern jazz musicians carry on this tradition of improvising. To improvise, a musician's grasp of music must go far beyond technical understanding. Jazz musicians must put a little of their own heart into what they play. If you have ever seen jazz musicians at work, you know that the effort and joy they put into their music is enormous. Two of the most famous jazz musicians are the trumpet players Louis Armstrong and Miles Davis.

Jazz is often upbeat. It reflects the musicians' joy in living. Have you ever heard the expression "Let's jazz this up"? To "jazz up" means to make something livelier. Even if you have never heard jazz played, you can imagine that it is anything but dreary!

Four to 10 musicians usually make up a jazz band. Besides the trumpet and clarinet, a jazz band may also include drums, piano, bass guitar, and sometimes a saxophone, violin and flute.

Directions: Answer these questions about jazz music.

1. What does **improvise** mean? _Make up your music_

2. Why did early jazz musicians improvise? _Because many black musicians didn't know how A to read_

3. Name two famous jazz musicians. _Louis Armstrong, Miles Davis_

4. Jazz music is ☐ slow. ☑ upbeat. ☐ dreary.

5. Which of the following is not a jazz instrument?

☐ drum ☐ piano ☑ organ ☐ violin ☐ flute

Name: _____

Recalling Details: Woodwinds

There are four kinds of woodwind instruments in modern bands. They are flutes, oboes, clarinets and bassoons. They are called "woodwind" instruments for two sensible reasons. In the beginning, they were all made of wood. Also, the musician's breath, or "wind," was required to play them.

Although they are all woodwinds, these instruments look different and are played differently. To play an oboe, the musician blows through a mouthpiece on the front of the instrument. The mouthpiece, called a reed, is made of two flat pieces of a kind of wood called cane. Clarinet players also blow into a reed mouthpiece. The clarinet has only one reed in its mouthpiece.

To play the flute, the musician blows across a hole near one end of the instrument. The way the breath is aimed helps to make the flute's different sounds. The bassoon is the largest woodwind instrument. Bassoon players blow through a mouthpiece that goes through a short metal pipe before it goes into the body of the bassoon. It makes a very different sound from the clarinet or the oboe.

Woodwind instruments also have keys—but not the kind of keys that open locks. These keys are more like levers that the musician pushes up and down. The levers cover holes. When the musician pushes down on a lever, it closes that hole. When he/she lifts his/her finger, it opens the hole. Different sounds are produced by controlling the amount of breath, or "wind," that goes through the holes.

Directions: Answer these questions about woodwind instruments.

1. What instruments are in the woodwind section? _Flutes, oboes, clarinets, bassoon_

2. Why are some instruments called woodwinds? _They are called wood-winds because they were made out of wood and you need to breath (wind)_

3. How is a flute different from the other woodwinds? _They have a different sound_

4. What happens when a musician pushes down on a woodwind key? _It makes a different sound_

5. How would a woodwind musician open the holes on his/her instrument?
They would to it while covering the whole hole

Name: _____

Comprehension: Harp Happenings

If you have ever heard a harpist play, you know what a lovely sound a harp makes. Music experts say the harp is among the oldest of instruments. It probably was invented several thousand years ago in or near Egypt.

The first harps are believed to have been made by stretching a string tightly between an empty tortoise shell and a curved pole. The empty shell magnified the sound the string made when it was plucked. More strings were added later so that more sounds could be made. Over the centuries, the shape of the harp gradually was changed into that of the large, graceful instruments we recognize today.

Here is how a harpist plays a harp. First, he/she leans the harp against his/her right shoulder. Then, the harpist puts his/her hands on either side of the harp and plucks its strings with both hands.

A harp has seven pedals on the bottom back. The audience usually cannot see these pedals. Most people are surprised to learn about them. The pedals are connected to the strings. Stepping on a particular pedal causes certain strings to tighten. The tightening and loosening of the strings makes different sounds; so does the way the strings are plucked with the hands.

At first glance, harps look like simple instruments. Actually, they are rather complicated and difficult to keep in tune. A harpist often spends as long as half an hour before a performance tuning his/her harp's strings so it produces the correct sounds.

Directions: Answer these questions about harps.

1. When were harps invented? _It was invented several thousand years_

2. Where were harps invented? _Harps were invented in Egypt_

3. What is a person called who plays the harp? _They're called a harpiest_

4. The harpist leans the harp against his/her

   ☒ right shoulder.   ☐ left shoulder.   ☐ left knee.

5. How many pedals does a harp have?

   ☐ five   ☐ six   ☒ seven

6. Harps are easy to play.

   ☐ yes   ☒ no

Name: _____

Comprehension: Brass Shows Class

If you like band music, you probably love the music made by brass instruments. Bright, loud, moving and magnificent—all these words describe the sounds made by brass.

Some of the earliest instruments were horns. Made from hollowed-out animal horns, these primitive instruments could not possibly have made the rich sounds of modern horns that are made of brass.

Most modern brass bands have three instruments—tubas, trombones and trumpets. Combined, these instruments can produce stirring marches, as well as haunting melodies. The most famous composer for brass instruments was John Phillip Sousa. Born in Washington, D.C., in 1854, Sousa was a military band conductor and composer. He died in 1932, but his music is still very popular today. One of Sousa's most famous tunes for military bands is "Stars and Stripes Forever."

Besides composing band music, Sousa also invented a practical band instrument—the sousaphone. The sousaphone is a huge tuba that makes very low noises. Because of the way it curls around the body, a sousaphone is easier to carry than a tuba, especially when the musician must march. This is exactly why John Phillip Sousa invented it!

Directions: Answer these questions about brass instruments.

1. Who invented the sousaphone? _John Phillip Sousa_

2. What were the first horns made from? _animal horns_

3. Where was John Phillip Sousa born? _1854_

4. When did John Phillip Sousa die? _1932_

5. Why did Sousa invent the sousaphone? _He invented it because its easy to carry Sousaphone_

6. What types of instruments make up a modern brass band? _Modern Brass instruments are tubas, trombones, and trumpets_

Comprehension: Violins

If you know anything about violin music, chances are you have heard the word **Stradivarius** (Strad-uh-vary-us). Stradivarius is the name for the world's most magnificent violins. They are named after their creator, Antonio Stradivari.

Stradivari was born in northern Italy and lived from 1644 to 1737. Cremona, the town he lived in, was a place where violins were manufactured. Stradivari was very young when he learned to play the violin. He grew to love the instrument so much that he began to make them himself.

Violins were new instruments during Stradivari's time. People made them in different sizes and shapes and of different types of wood. Stradivari is said to have been very particular about the wood he selected for his violins. He took long walks alone in the forest to find just the right tree. He is also said to have used a secret and special type of varnish to put on the wood. Whatever the reasons, his violins are the best in the world.

Stradivari put such care and love into his violins that they are still used today. Many of these are in museums. But some wealthy musicians, who can afford the thousands and thousands of dollars they cost, own Stradivarius violins.

Stradivari passed his methods on to his sons. But the secrets of making Stradivarius violins seem to have died out with the family. Their rarity, as well as their mellow sound, make Stradivarius violins among the most prized instruments in the world.

Directions: Answer these questions about Stradivarius violins.

1. Where did Stradivari live? _In Northen Italy_

2. Why did he begin making violins? _He grew to love them so he made them_

3. Why are Stradivarius violins special? _The are special because they are made carefully and can last long_

4. Where can Stradivarius violins be found today? _They can be found in museums and people who can afford them_

5. How did Stradivari select the wood for his violins? _He selected it by taking long walks in the woods_

6. Who else knew Stradivari's secrets for making such superior violins?
His sons new his secrets

19

Name: Lauren

Review

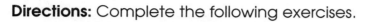

Directions: Complete the following exercises.

1. Write a four-sentence summary of the selection "Where Did Songs Come From?" (page 12).

    Songs came from people from long ago who belived there were various gods that lived in the sky so they sange songs to respect the gods

2. Describe the main difference between a clarinet and an oboe.

    The main diffrence is the reed the and mouth piece

3. How do the keys of woodwind instruments work?

    The keys of the wood winds are holes that are covered by your fingers

4. Write a summary of the history of the harp.

    The harp was made several years ago by the egyptions. There are seven pedals on a harp. People who play harps are harpiests

5. Define the following words from the selection "Facts About Folk Music" (page 13).

    verses: the lines of the song

    excavating: looking for

    chariot: a carrige

    composed: the person who made the song

Name: _____

Using Prior Knowledge: Farm Animals

Directions: Before reading about farm animals in the following section, answer these questions.

1. List at least nine types of farm animals by mother and baby names.

   Example: sow—piglet.

   Cow - calf   Sow-piglet   Duck- Duckling
   Chicken-chick   Dog-puppy   _____
   Sheep- Lamb   Cat-kitten   _____

2. If you owned a large ranch, what type of livestock would you enjoy keeping? Why?

   I would enjoy horses, cows, bulls, hens, and
   pigs.

3. Some animals routinely give birth to twins, triplets or larger litters. Which animals give birth to more than one baby at a time?

   pigs, chickens, and Ducks

4. Would you enjoy living on a farm? Why or why not?

   I wouldn't because it is far away from
   citys and other things I would wanna have

5. What is the importance of raising livestock today?

   The importance is to provide meat for
   people

Sequencing: "Little Bo-Peep"

Sequencing means placing events or objects in the correct order.

Directions: Read "Little Bo-Peep." Then number the events in the poem in the correct order.

Little Bo-Peep has lost her sheep,
And can't tell where to find them.
"I'll leave them alone, and they'll come home,
Wagging their tails behind them."

Then Little Bo-Peep dreamed of her sheep,
She dreamed she heard the bleating.
But when she awoke, she found it a joke,
For they were still a-fleeting.

Then up she took her little crook,
Determined for to find them.
She found them indeed,
But it made her heart bleed,
For they'd left their tails behind them!

It happened one day that Bo-Peep did stray
Into a meadow nearby,
She looked up in a tree, and what did she see?
Their tails all hung out to dry!

Bo-Peep heaved a sigh and looked to the sky
As she gathered their tails up fast.
She ran to her sheep, they all gave a bleat
And said, "Our tails are back at last!"

__6__ Little Bo-Peep returned her sheep's tails to them.

__2__ Little Bo-Peep decided her sheep would find their way home.

__1__ Little Bo-Peep lost her sheep.

__3__ Little Bo-Peep dreamed about her sheep.

__5__ Little Bo-Peep found her sheep.

__4__ Little Bo-Peep found her sheeps' tails in a tree.

Name: _____

Comprehension: All About Sheep

Did you ever wonder what really happened to the tails of Little Bo-Peep's sheep? Here's the real story.

When sheep are born, they are called lambs. Lambs are born with long tails. A few days after lambs are born, the shepherd cuts off their tails. Because they get dirty, the lambs' long tails can pick up lots of germs. Cutting them off helps to prevent disease. The procedure is called "docking." This is probably what happened to Bo-Peep's sheep! Another shepherd must have cut their tails off without telling her.

Little lambs are cute. A lamb grows inside its mother for 150 days before it is born. This is called the "gestation period." Some types of sheep, such as hill sheep, give birth to one lamb at a time. Other types of sheep, such as lowland sheep, give birth to two or three lambs at a time.

After it is born, it takes a lamb 3 or 4 days to recognize its mother. Once it does, it stays close to her until it is about 3 weeks old. After that, the lamb becomes friendly toward other lambs.

Young lambs then form play groups. They chase each other in circles. They butt into each other. Like children, they pretend to fight. When play gets too rough, the lambs run back to their mothers for protection.

Lambs follow their mothers as they graze on grass. Usually, sheep move in single file behind an older female sheep. Female sheep are called ewes. The ewes teach their lambs how to keep themselves clean. This is called "grooming." Sheep groom only their faces. Here is how they do it: They lick one of their front legs, then they rub their faces against the spot they have licked.

Directions: Follow the instructions below.

1. Define the word **docking**. _Docking means the procedure of having a lamb_

2. Name a type of sheep that gives birth to one lamb at a time. _Hill sheep_

3. Name a type of sheep that gives birth to two or three lambs at a time.

lowland sheep

4. Female sheep are called

☐ grazers. ☒ ewes. ☐ dockers.

5. Lambs begin playing in groups when they are

☐ 2 weeks old. ☒ 3 weeks old. ☐ 4 weeks old.

Name: _____

Recalling Details: "Little Boy Blue"

Directions: Read "Little Boy Blue." Then complete the puzzle.

Little Boy Blue, come blow your horn.

The sheep's in the meadow, the cow's in the corn;

But where is the boy who looks after the sheep?

He's under a haystack, fast asleep!

Will you awake him? No, not I.

For if I do, he's sure to cry.

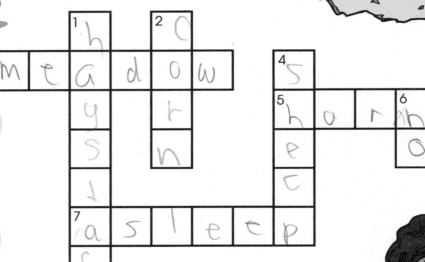

Across:

3. This is where the sheep was.

5. What Little Boy Blue was asked to blow.

7. The other boy was fast _____.

8. Little Boy Blue was not asleep. He was _____.

Down:

1. The boy who looks after the sheep slept here.

2. This is what the cow got into.

4. This is what the boy was supposed to be tending.

6. Did they wake the sleeping boy?

Name: _____

Comprehension: Pigs Are Particular

Have you ever wondered why pigs wallow in the mud? It's not because they are dirty animals. Pigs have no sweat glands. They can't sweat, so they roll in the mud to cool themselves. The next time you hear anyone who's hot say, "I'm sweating like a pig!" be sure to correct him/her. Humans can sweat but pigs cannot.

Actually, pigs are particular about their pens. They are very clean animals. They prefer to sleep in clean, dry places. They move their bowels and empty their bladders in another area. They do not want to get their homes dirty.

Another misconception about pigs is that they are smooth. Only cartoon pigs are pink, smooth and shiny-looking. The skin of real pigs is covered with bristles—small, stiff hairs. Their bristles protect their tender skin. When pigs are slaughtered, their bristles are sometimes made into hair brushes or clothes brushes.

Female pigs are called sows. Sows have babies twice a year and give birth to 10 to 14 piglets at a time. The babies have a "gestation period" of 16 weeks before they are born.

All the piglets together are called a "litter." Newborn piglets are on their tiny feet within a few minutes after birth. Can you guess why? They are hungrily looking for their mother's teats so they can get milk. As they nurse, piglets snuggle in close to their mother's belly to keep warm.

Directions: Answer these questions about pigs.

1. Why do pigs wallow in mud? _They wallow in the mud because they don't have sweat glands the mud cools them off_

2. How long is the gestation period for pigs? _____

3. What are pig bristles used for? _Their used for brushes and clouths_

4. Tell two reasons pigs are on their feet soon after they are born.

1) _To eat_   2) _to snuggle_

5. A female pig is called a

   ☐ bristle.   ☐ piglet.   ☒ sow.

6. Together, the newborn piglets are called a

   ☐ group.   ☐ family.   ☒ litter.

© 1999 American Education Publishing Co.

Name: _____

Context Clues: No Kidding About Goats

Goats are independent creatures. Unlike sheep, which move easily in herds, goats cannot be driven along by a goatherd. They must be moved one or two at a time. Moving a big herd of goats can take a long time, so goatherds must be patient people.

Both male and female goats can have horns, but some goats don't have them at all. Male goats have beards but females do not. Male goats also have thicker and shaggier coats than females. During breeding season, when goats mate to produce babies, male goats have a very strong smell.

Goats are kept in paddocks with high fences. The fences are high because goats are good jumpers. They like to nibble on hedges and on the tips of young trees. They can cause a lot of damage this way! That is why many farmers keep their goats in a paddock.

Baby goats are called "kids," and two or three at a time are born to the mother goat. Farmers usually begin to bottle-feed kids when they are a few days old. They milk the mother goat and keep the milk. Goat's milk is much easier to digest than cow's milk, and many people think it tastes delicious.

Directions: Answer these questions about goats.

1. Use context clues to choose the correct definition of **goatherd**.

   ☒ person who herds goats   ☐ goats in a herd   ☐ person who has heard of goats

2. Use context clues to choose the correct definition of **paddock**.

   ☐ pad   ☐ fence   ☒ pen

3. Use context clues to choose the correct definition of **nibble**.

   ☒ take small bites   ☐ take small drinks   ☐ take little sniffs

4. Use context clues to choose the correct definition of **delicious**.

   ☐ delicate   ☒ tasty   ☐ terrible

Name: _____

Comprehension: Cows Are Complicated

If you believe cows have four stomachs, you're right! It sounds incredible, but it's true.

Here are the "hows" and "whys" of a cow's digestive system. First, it's important to know that cows do not have front teeth. They eat grass by wrapping their tongues around it and pulling it from the ground. They do have back teeth, but still they cannot properly chew the grass.

Cows swallow grass without chewing it. When it's swallowed, the grass goes into the cow's first stomach, called a "rumen" (roo-mun). There it is broken up by the digestive juices and forms into a ball of grass. This ball is called a "cud." The cow is able to bring the cud back up into its mouth. Then the cow chews the cud into a pulp with its back teeth and re-swallows it.

After it is swallowed the second time, the cud goes into the cow's second stomach. This second stomach is called the "reticulum" (re-tick-u-lum). The reticulum filters the food to sort out any small stones or other non-food matter. Then it passes the food onto the cow's third stomach. The third stomach is called the "omasum" (oh-mass-um).

From there, any food that is still undigested is sent back to the first stomach so the cow can bring it back up into her mouth and chew it some more. The rest goes into the cow's fourth stomach. The fourth stomach is called the "abomasum" (ab-oh-ma-sum). Digesting food that can be turned into milk is a full-time job for cows!

Directions: Answer these questions about cows.

1. List in order the names of a cow's four stomachs.

1) ___rumen___ 2) ___reticulum___ 3) ___onasum___ 4) ___abomasum___

2. What is the name of the ball of grass a cow chews on? _____ cud

3. A cow has no

☒ front teeth.   ☐ back teeth.   ☐ fourth stomach.

4. Which stomach acts as a filter for digestion?

☒ reticulum   ☐ rumen   ☐ abomasum

Name: _____

Context Clues: Dairy Cows

Some cows are raised for their beef. Other cows, called dairy cows, are raised for their milk. A dairy cow cannot produce any milk until after its first calf is born. Cows are not mature enough to give birth until they are 2 years old. A cow's gestation period is 40 weeks long, and she usually gives birth to one calf. Then she produces a lot of milk to feed it. When the calf is 2 days old, the dairy farmer takes the calf away from its mother. After that, the cow is milked twice a day.

The dairy cow's milk comes from the large, smooth udder beneath her body. The udder has four openings called "teats." To milk the cow, the farmer grasps a teat and squeezes it with his thumb and forefinger. Then he gently but firmly pulls his hand down the teat to squeeze the milk out. Milking machines that are hooked to the cow's teats duplicate this action and can milk many cows quickly.

A dairy cow's milk production is not at the same level all the time. When the cow is pregnant, milk production gradually decreases. For 2 months before her calf is born, a cow is said to be "dry" and is not milked. This happens because, like humans, much of the cow's food is actually being used to nourish the unborn calf.

Farmers give the cow extra food at this time to make sure the mother and unborn calf are well-nourished. Again, like humans, well-nourished mother cows are more likely to produce healthy babies.

Directions: Answer these questions about dairy cows.

1. Use context clues to choose the correct definition of **grasp**.

☐ pull firmly ☒ hold firmly ☐ hold gently

2. Use context clues to choose the correct definition of **duplicate**.

☐ correct ☐ make ☒ copy

3. Use context clues to choose the correct definition of **decrease**.

☐ become more ☒ become less ☐ become quicker

4. Use context clues to choose the correct definition of **nourish**.

☐ to be happy ☐ to be friendly ☒ to feed

Name: _____

Comprehension: Chickens

Have you ever heard the expression "pecking order"? In the pecking order of a school, the principal is at the top of the order. Next comes the assistant principal, then the teachers and students.

In the pecking order of chickens, the most aggressive chicken is the leader. The leader is the hen that uses her beak most often to peck the chickens she bosses. These chickens, in turn, boss other chickens by pecking them, and so on. Chickens can peck all others who are "below" them in the pecking order. They never peck "above" themselves by pecking their bosses.

Answer these questions about chickens.

1. Put this pecking order of four chickens in order.

_____ This chicken pecks numbers 3 and 4 but never 1.

_____ No one pecks this chicken. She's the top boss.

_____ This chicken can't peck anyone.

_____ This chicken pecks chicken number 4.

2. Use context clues to figure out the definition of **aggressive**. _Means that it is frightful_

_____

3. Who is at the top of the pecking order in a school? _The leader_

_____

Review

Directions: Follow the instructions for each section.

1. Write a summary of the selection "All About Sheep" (page 23).

   Sheep are white wooly animals. There
   are two types Hill sheep and lowland sheep. The babies are called lambs

2. What is the purpose of a pig's bristles?

   The purpose is to make brushes
   and brushes for clouthing.

3. Write a summary of the selection "No Kidding About Goats" (page 26).

   Goats are Independent creatures
   Both male and female can have horns
   Males have beards, females do not

4. What is the purpose of a cow's four stomachs?

   The purpose is so with all the
   food the cow eats, its all turned
   into milk

5. How do chickens establish leaders and followers?

   They establish leaders by who pecks the
   most

6. What is a "cud"?

   A ball of grass a cow chews

Name: _Lauren_

Review

Directions: Define the following words from this section.

1. bleating: _____

2. graze: _To walk around_____

3. wallow: _____

4. gestation: _____

5. independent: _____

6. paddock: _Caral_____

7. digest: _eat_____

8. rumen: _____

9. reticulum: _____

10. omasum: _____

11. abomasum: _____

12. pulp: _____

13. duplicate: _More than one_____

14. nourish: _____

15. aggressive: _initiated to fight_____

Directions: Choose four words from above and use each in a sentence.

1. _____

2. _____

3. _____

4. _____

Using Prior Knowledge: Books

Directions: Before reading about books in the following section, answer these questions.

1. What books have you read recently?

The Bad Beggining

_____

2. Write a summary of one of the books you listed above.

The Bad Beggining is about 3 children who are orphans. They go to a foster home but they don't like it there. They were left with a big amount of money. Their foster parent wants the money so they have to think of a plan to stop him

3. Define the following types of books and, if possible, give an example of each.

biography: A book about someone

_____

fiction: Something that is made up

_____

mystery: A book about a case where you don't know who did what

nonfiction: Nonfiction is true stories

_____

Context Clues: Remember Who You Are

Directions: Read each paragraph. Then use context clues to figure out the meanings of the bold words.

During the 1940s, Esther Hautzig lived in the town of Vilna, which was then part of Poland. Shortly after the **outbreak** of World War II, she and her family were **deported** to Siberia by Russian communists who hated Jews. She told what happened to her and other Polish Jews in a book. The book is called *Remember Who You Are: Stories About Being Jewish*.

1. Choose the correct definition of **deported**.

   ☒ sent away   ☐ asked to go   ☐ invited to visit

2. Choose the correct definition of **outbreak**.

   ☒ a sudden occurrence   ☐ to leave suddenly

Remember Who You Are: Stories About Being Jewish is a nonfiction book that tells true stories. An interesting **fiction** book is *Leave the Cooking to Me* by Judie Angell. It tells the story of a girl named Shirley, who learns about cooking from her best friend's mother. Shirley gets very good at making fancy food. Most young people have a hard time finding jobs that pay well, but Shirley's cooking skills help her land a **lucrative** summer job.

3. Choose the correct definition of **fiction**.

   ☐ stories that are true   ☒ stories that are not true

4. Choose the correct definition of **lucrative**.

   ☒ interesting   ☐ profitable   ☐ nearby

Comprehension: Books and More Books!

Variety is said to be the spice of life. Where books are concerned, variety is the key to reading pleasure. There is a type of book that appeals to every reader.

Each year, hundreds of new books are published for children. A popular series of books for girls between the ages of 8 and 12 is *Sweet Valley Kids*, written by Francine Pascal. All of Pascal's books are fictional stories about children who live in the town of Sweet Valley.

If you like legends, an interesting book is *Dream Wolf* by Paul Goble. *Dream Wolf* is a retelling of an old Native American legend. Legends are stories passed down from one generation to another that may or may not be true. Some of them are scary! *The Legend of Sleepy Hollow*, for example, is about a headless horseman. Other legends are about a person's brave or amazing deeds. For example, there are many legends about Robin Hood, who stole from the rich and gave to the poor.

Many people like to read nonfiction books, which are about things that really exist or really happened. Many children who like nonfiction choose books about animals, careers, sports and hobbies. Those interested in information about Native Americans might like to read these books: *The Navajos* by Peter Iverson, *The Yakima* by Helen Schuster and *The Creek* by Michael Green. The titles of these nonfiction books are names of Native American tribes.

Directions: Answer these questions about different types of books.

1. What is the name of Francine Pascal's book series? _Sweet Valley Kids_

2. What legend is about a headless horseman? _The Legend of Sleepy Hollow_

3. Which of the following is not correct about legends?

☐ Legends are passed down through the generations.

☒ All legends are scary.

☐ Some legends are about people who did braves things.

Name: _____

Comprehension: Help for the Homeless

In Dayton, Ohio, a bookstore called Books & Co. launched a program to educate the public about the needs of homeless people. The program was built around profits from sales of a book called *Louder Than Words*. The book is a collection of 22 short stories by such noted authors as Louise Erdrich and Anne Tyler.

Many of the authors helped promote the book by coming to the bookstore to autograph copies of *Louder Than Words*. All profits from the sale of the book were donated to a fund that provides food and housing for homeless people.

The fund for the homeless is managed by a nonprofit organization called Share Our Strength. Located in Washington, D.C., the organization distributes the money to food banks and shelters for homeless people around the United States.

By the end of 1990, $50,000 had been raised for the homeless from the sale of *Louder Than Words*. Other bookstore owners learned about the success of Books & Co. in raising money for the homeless. They were impressed! Now, bookstores in these other cities are running fund-raising efforts of their own: Ann Arbor, Michigan; Columbus, Ohio; Taos, New Mexico; and Minneapolis, Minnesota.

Directions: Answer these questions about how booksellers have helped raise funds for the homeless.

1. How many short stories are in the book *Louder Than Words*? __22__

2. What is the name of the organization that distributes money to homeless shelters
   around the country? __Louder than words__

3. Name two authors whose stories are included in *Louder Than Words*.

   __Louise Erdich, Anne Tyler__

4. Share Our Strength is located in what city?

   ☐ Portland, OR   ☐ Minneapolis, MN   ☒ Washington, D.C.

5. In what city is Books & Co. located?

   ☐ Columbus, OH   ☒ Dayton, OH   ☐ Taos, NM

Name: _____

Fact or Opinion?

Directions: Read the paragraphs below. Then, in the corresponding numbered blanks, write whether each numbered sentence is a fact or an opinion.

Have you ever seen *Reading Rainbow* on your local public television station? **(1)** It's a show about books, and its host is LeVar Burton. **(2)** LeVar is very handsome and the show is great!

Some books that have been featured on the show are *I Can Be an Oceanographer* by Paul Sipiera, *Soccer Sam* by Jean Marzolla, *Redbird* by Patrick Fort and *Miss Nelson Has a Field Day* by Harry Allard. **(3)** *Miss Nelson Has a Field Day* sounds like the most interesting book of all!

(4) On *Reading Rainbow,* children give informal book reports about books they have read. **(5)** All the children are adorable! In about 1 minute, each child describes his or her book. **(6)** While the child is talking, pictures of some of the pages from the book are shown. **(7)** Seeing the pictures will make you want to read the book. A few books are described on each show. **(8)** Other activities include trips with LeVar to places the books tell about. **(9)** Every child should make time to watch *Reading Rainbow*! **(10)** It's a fabulous show!

1. _Fact_
2. _Opinion_
3. _Opinion_
4. _Fact_
5. _Opinion_
6. _Fact_
7. _Opinion_
8. _Opinion_
9. _Opinion_
10. _Opinion_

Name: _____

Context Clues: Kids' Books Are Big Business

Between 1978 and 1988, the number of children's books published in the United States doubled. The publishing industry, which prints, promotes and sells books, does not usually move this fast. Why? Because if publishers print too many books that don't sell, they lose money. They like to wait, if they can, to see what the "public demand" is for certain types of books. Then they accept manuscripts from writers who have written the types of books the public seems to want. More than 4,600 children's books were published in 1988, because publishers thought they could sell that many titles. Many copies of each title were printed and sold to bookstores and libraries. The publishers made good profits and, since then, the number of children's books published each year has continued to grow.

The title of a recent new book for children is *The Wild Horses of Sweetbriar* by Natalie Kinsey-Warnock. It is the story of a girl and a band of wild horses that lived on an island off the coast of Massachusetts in 1903. The story sounds very exciting! Wild horses can be quite dangerous. The plot of *The Wild Horses of Sweetbriar* is probably filled with danger and suspense.

Directions: Answer these questions about how interest in writing, reading and selling children's books has grown.

1. Use context clues to choose the correct definition of **industry**.

   ☐ booksellers   ☐ writers   ☒ entire business

2. If 4,600 books were sold in 1988, how many books were sold in 1978? _____

3. The number of children's books published
   in the United States doubled between 1978 and 1988.   (Fact)   Opinion

4. *The Wild Horses of Sweetbriar* is the story of a girl and a
   band of wild horses that lived on an island in 1903.   (Fact)   Opinion

5. The story sounds very exciting!   Fact   (Opinion)

6. The plot of *The Wild Horses of Sweetbriar* is probably
   filled with danger and suspense.   Fact   (Opinion)

Review

Directions: Follow the instructions below.

1. Write a summary of the selection "Help for the Homeless" (page 35).

   Help for the Homeless is for raising money for poor people by selling books with autographs on them.

2. What skills must a writer have in order to produce a book?

   Writers must have the a good imagination for writing stories

3. Define the following words from this section.

   appeal: to standout

   legend: A story passed down from generations

   deed: A action that helps

   generation: a series of years

   profit: an amount of money

   distribute: to give out

   suspense: _____

   manuscript: _____

4. Interview the members of your family. Ask each person his/her favorite book title and the reason he/she enjoyed it. Then, summarize your findings in a paragraph.

   _____

   _____

   _____

   _____

Using Prior Knowledge: Cooking

Before reading about cooking in the following section, answer these questions.

1. What is your favorite recipe? Why?

Pizza is my favorite recipe because it is
my favorite food and it is fun to make.

2. What do you most like to cook? Why?

Pizza because I like making it.

3. Have you tried food from cultures other than your own? If so, which type of food do you like most? Why?

No, I have not

4. Why is it important to follow the correct sequence when preparing a recipe?

It is importent because if you do one
thing wrong it could ruin your recipe

5. What safety precautions must be followed when working in a kitchen?

A big safety precaution that must be
followed is you should be carefull with
electricity

Following Directions: Chunky Tomato and Green Onion Sauce

Following directions means to do what the directions say to do, step by step, in the correct order.

Directions: Read the recipe for chunky tomato and green onion sauce. Answer the questions below.

Ingredients:

- 2 tablespoons corn oil

- 2 cloves of garlic, finely chopped

- $1\frac{1}{2}$ pounds plum tomatoes, cored, peeled, seeded, then coarsely chopped

- 3 green onions, cut in half lengthwise, then thinly sliced

- salt

- freshly ground pepper

Heat oil in a heavy skillet over medium heat. Add garlic and cook until yellow, about 1 minute. Stir in tomatoes. Season with salt and pepper. Cook until thickened, about 10 minutes. Stir in green onions and serve.

1. What is the last thing the cook does to prepare the tomatoes before cooking them?

   Stir in green onions

2. What kind of oil does the cook heat in the heavy skillet? _Corn oil_

3. How long should the garlic be cooked? _I minute_

4. What does the cook do to the tomatoes right before removing the seeds?

   pealed and chopped

5. Is the sauce served hot or cold? _hot_

Comprehension: Cooking With Care

People are so busy these days that many have no time to cook. This creates a problem, because most families love home cooking! The food tastes good and warm, and a family meal brings everyone together. In some families, meals are often the only times everyone sees one another at the same time.

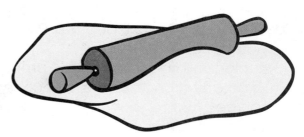

Another reason people enjoy home cooking is that it is often a way of showing love. A parent who bakes a batch of chocolate chip cookies isn't just satisfying a child's sweet tooth. He/she is sending a message. The message says, "I care about you enough to spend an hour making cookies that you will eat up in 15 minutes if I let you!"

There's also something about the smell of good cooking that appeals to people of all ages. It makes most of us feel secure and loved—even if we are the ones doing the cooking! Next time you smell a cake baking, stop for a moment and pay attention to your mood. Chances are, the good smell is making you feel happy.

Real estate agents know that good cooking smells are important. They sometimes advise people whose homes are for sale to bake cookies or bread if prospective buyers are coming to see the house. The good smells make the place "feel like home." These pleasant smells help convince potential buyers that the house would make a good home for their family, too!

Directions: Answer these questions about good cooking.

1. Why do fewer people cook nowadays? _Yes, fewer people cook nowadays_

2. Why are family meals important? _Family meals are important because they bring people together_

3. What do homemade cookies do besides satisfy a child's sweet tooth?

They make the child feel more at home.

4. Real estate agents often advise home sellers holding open houses to

☐ clean the garage. ☒ bake cookies or bread.

5. The smell of baking at open houses may encourage buyers to

☐ bake cookies. ☒ buy the house. ☐ bake bread.

Sequencing: Chocolate Chunk Cookies

These chocolate chunk cookies require only five ingredients. Before you combine them, preheat the oven to 350 degrees. Preheating the oven to the correct temperature is always step number one in baking.

Now, into a large mixing bowl, empty an $18\frac{1}{4}$-ounce package of chocolate fudge cake mix (any brand). Add a 10-ounce package of semi-sweet chocolate, broken into small pieces, two $5\frac{1}{8}$-ounce packages of chocolate fudge pudding mix (any brand) and $1\frac{1}{2}$ cups chopped walnuts.

Use a large wooden spoon to combine the ingredients. When they are well-mixed, add $1\frac{1}{2}$ cups mayonnaise and stir thoroughly. Shape the dough into small balls and place the balls 2 inches apart on an ungreased cookie sheet. Bake 12 minutes. Cool and eat!

Directions: Number in correct order the steps for making chocolate chunk cookies.

_____7_____ Place $1\frac{1}{2}$ cups of mayonnaise in the bowl.

_____8_____ Shape dough into small balls and place them on a cookie sheet.

_____2_____ Empty the package of chocolate fudge cake mix into the bowl.

_____9_____ Bake the dough for 12 minutes.

_____4_____ Place two $5\frac{1}{8}$-ounce packages of chocolate fudge pudding in the bowl.

_____5_____ Put $1\frac{1}{2}$ cups chopped walnuts in the bowl.

_____1_____ Preheat the oven to 350 degrees.

_____3_____ Place the 10-ounce package of semi-sweet chocolate pieces in the bowl.

_____6_____ Stir everything thoroughly.

Comprehension: Eating High-Fiber Foods

Have you heard your parents or other adults talk about "high-fiber" diets? Foods that are high in fiber, like oats and other grains, are believed to be very healthy. Here's why: The fiber adds bulk to the food the body digests and helps keep the large intestines working properly. Corn, apples, celery, nuts and other chewy foods also contain fiber that helps keep the body's systems for digesting and eliminating food working properly.

Researchers at the University of Minnesota have found another good reason to eat high-fiber food, especially at breakfast. Because fiber is bulky, it absorbs a lot of liquid in the stomach. As it absorbs the liquid, it swells. This "fools" the stomach into thinking it's full. As a result, when lunchtime comes, those who have eaten a high-fiber breakfast are not as hungry. They eat less food at lunch. Without much effort on their parts, dieters eating a high-fiber breakfast can lose weight.

The university researchers say a person could lose 10 pounds in a year just by eating a high-fiber breakfast! This is good news to people who are only slightly overweight and want an easy method for losing that extra 10 pounds.

Directions: Answer these questions about eating high-fiber foods.

1. Why is fiber healthy? _Fiber is healthy because_ _____

_____

2. How does fiber "fool" the stomach? _____

_____

3. How does "fooling" the stomach help people lose weight? _____

_____

4. How many pounds could a dieter eating a high-fiber breakfast lose in a year?

☐ 20 pounds   ☐ 30 pounds   ☐ 10 pounds

5. The university that did the research is in which state?

☐ Michigan   ☐ Minnesota   ☐ Montana

Main Idea: New Corn

I will clothe myself in spring clothing

And visit the slopes of the eastern hill.

By the mountain stream, a mist hovers,

Hovers a moment and then scatters.

Then comes a wind blowing from the south

That brushes the fields of new corn.

Directions: Answer these questions about this ancient poem, which is translated from Chinese.

1. Circle the main idea:

   The poet will dress comfortably and go to where the corn grows so he/she can enjoy the beauty of nature.

   The poet will dress comfortably and visit the slopes of the eastern hill, where he/she will plant corn.

2. From which direction does the wind blow? _____

3. Where does the mist hover? _____

4. What do you think the poet means by "spring clothing"? _____

_____

Comprehension: The French Eat Differently

Many people believe that French people are very different from Americans. This is certainly true where eating habits are concerned! According to a report by the World Health Organization, each year the French people eat four times more butter than Americans. The French also eat twice as much cheese! In addition, they eat more vegetables, potatoes, grain and fish.

Yet, despite the fact that they eat larger amounts of these foods, the French take in about the same number of calories each day as Americans. (French and American men consume about 2,500 calories daily. French and American women take in about 1,600 calories daily.)

How can this be? If the French are eating more of certain types of foods, shouldn't this add up to more calories? And why are so few French people overweight compared to Americans? The answer—Americans consume 18 times more refined sugar than the French and drink twice as much whole milk!

Although many Americans believe the French end each meal with grand and gooey desserts, this just isn't so. Except for special occasions, dessert in a typical French home consists of fresh fruit or cheese. Many American families, on the other hand, like to end their meals with a bowl or two of ice cream or another sweet treat.

It's believed that this difference in the kind of calories consumed—rather than in the total number of calories taken in—is what causes many Americans to be chubby and most French people to be thin.

Directions: Answer these questions about the eating habits of French and American people.

1. How many calories does the average French man eat each day? _____

2. How much whole milk does the average French person drink compared to the average

American? _____

3. How much more refined sugar do Americans eat than the French?

☐ 2 times more   ☐ 18 times more   ☐ 15 times more

4. What do French families usually eat for dessert?

☐ refined sugar   ☐ ice cream   ☐ fruit and cheese

Comprehension: Chinese Cabbage

Many Americans enjoy Chinese food. In big cities, like New York and Chicago, many Chinese restaurants deliver their food in small boxes to homes. It's just like ordering a pizza! Then the people who ordered the "take-out" food simply open it, put it on their plates and eat it while it's hot.

Because it tastes so good, many people are curious about the ingredients in Chinese food. Siu choy and choy sum are two types of Chinese cabbage that many people enjoy eating. Siu choy grows to be 2 to 3 feet! Of course, it is chopped into small pieces before it is cooked and served. Its leaves are light green and soft. It is not crunchy like American cabbage. Siu choy is used in soups and stews. Sometimes it is pickled with vinegar and other ingredients and served as a side dish to other courses.

Choy sum looks and tastes different from siu choy. Choy sum grows to be only 8 to 10 inches. It is a flowering cabbage that grows small yellow flowers. The flowers are "edible," which means they can be eaten. Its leaves are long and bright green. After its leaves are boiled for 4 minutes, choy sum is often served as a salad. Oil and oyster sauce are mixed together and poured over choy sum as a salad dressing.

Directions: Answer these questions about Chinese cabbage.

1. Which Chinese cabbage grows small yellow flowers?_____

2. Which Chinese cabbage is served as a salad?_____

3. Is siu choy crunchy? _____

4. What ingredients are in the salad dressing used on choy sum?

_____

5. To what size does siu choy grow? _____

6. Name two main dishes in which siu choy is used. _____

Name: _____

Review

Here's a recipe for a special mashed potato treat that serves two people. The recipe is fast and easy to follow, and the results are delicious!

Begin by peeling two large potatoes and cooking them in a pot of boiling water. When a fork or knife inserted into them pulls out easily, you will know they are done. Then take them from the pot and drain them well. Place them in a large mixing bowl and add 2 tablespoons of milk and 2 tablespoons of butter. Mash with a potato masher until the lumps are gone.

In a skillet, melt a tablespoon of butter and add one bunch of chopped green onions. Cook them about 1 minute. Add them to the potatoes and mix gently. Season with salt and pepper and add more butter if desired. Serve and eat!

Directions: Answer these questions about how to make mashed potatoes with green onions.

1. Circle the main idea:

   This recipe is fast and easy, and the potatoes are delicious.

   This recipe has only four ingredients (plus salt and pepper).

2. Name the main ingredients in this recipe (not including salt and pepper).

   _____

3. How many people does this recipe serve? _____

4. Number in order the steps for making mashed potatoes with green onions.

   _____ Cook the chopped green onions for 1 minute.

   _____ Peel two potatoes.

   _____ Season with salt and pepper and serve.

   _____ Put the cooked potatoes in a bowl with milk and butter, then mash.

   _____ Add the onions to the mashed potatoes.

   _____ Boil the potatoes until they are done.

Name: _____

Using Prior Knowledge: Greek and Roman Mythology

Directions: Before reading about Greek and Roman mythology in the following section, answer these questions.

1. Hercules is a man from Greek and Roman mythology. Write a short paragraph describing what you know about Hercules.

   _____

   _____

   _____

2. Can you think of anything today that derived its name from a Greek or Roman myth?

   _____

   _____

   _____

3. Compare and contrast what you know of Greek and Roman beliefs about mythology with your beliefs.

   _____

   _____

   _____

   _____

   _____

   _____

4. Many constellations are named after gods, goddesses and mythical creatures. Name at least six.

   _____   _____   _____

   _____   _____   _____

Comprehension: Roman Legends

Long ago, people did not know as much about science and astronomy as they do today. When they did not understand something, they thought the "gods" were responsible. The ancient Romans believed there were many gods and that each god or goddess (a female god) was responsible for certain things.

For example, the Romans believed Ceres (Sir-eez) was the goddess who made flowers, plants, trees and other things grow. She was a lot like what people today refer to as Mother Nature. Ceres was also responsible for the good weather that made crops grow. You can see why Ceres was such an important goddess to the ancient Romans.

Apollo was the god of the sun. People believed he used his chariot to pull the sun up each day and take it down at night. Apollo was extremely good-looking. His home was a golden palace near the sun surrounded by fluffy white clouds. Apollo had to work every single day, but he lived a wonderful life.

Jupiter was the most important god of all. He was the god who ruled all of the other gods, as well as the people. Jupiter was also called Jove. Maybe you have heard someone use the exclamation, "By Jove!" That person is talking about Jupiter! The word **father** is derived from the word **Jupiter**. Although he did not really exist, Jupiter influenced our language.

Directions: Answer these questions about Roman legends.

1. What imaginary figure is Ceres compared to today? _____

2. Where did Apollo live? _____

3. The word **father** is derived from the name of this god:

☐ Ceres   ☐ Apollo   ☐ Jupiter

4. Which is not true of Apollo?   ☐ He had to work every day.

☐ He lived in a mountain cave.

☐ He was very handsome.

Name: _____

Comprehension: Apollo and Phaethon

Apollo, the sun god, had a son named Phaethon (Fay-a-thun). Like most boys, Phaethon was proud of his father. He liked to brag to his friends about Apollo's important job, but no one believed that the great Apollo was his father.

Phaethon thought of a way to prove to his friends that he was telling the truth. He went to Apollo and asked if he could drive the chariot of the sun. If his friends saw him making the sun rise and set, they would be awestruck!

Apollo did not want to let Phaethon drive the chariot. He was afraid Phaethon was not strong enough to control the horses. But Phaethon begged until Apollo gave in. "Stay on the path," Apollo said. "If you dip too low, the sun will catch the earth on fire. If you go too high, people will freeze."

Unfortunately, Apollo's worst fears came true. Phaethon could not control the horses. He let them pull the chariot of the sun too close to the earth. To keep the earth from burning, Jupiter, father of the gods, sent a thunderbolt that hit Phaethon and knocked him from the driver's seat. When Phaethon let go of the reins, the horses pulled the chariot back up onto the proper path. Phaethon was killed as he fell to earth. His body caught fire and became a shooting star.

Directions: Answer these questions about the Roman legend of Apollo and his son.

1. Who did not believe Apollo was Phaethon's father? _____

2. What did Phaethon do to prove Apollo was his father? _____

_____

3. Why did Jupiter send a lightning bolt? _____

_____

4. Which was not a warning from Apollo to Phaethon?

☐ Don't go too close to the earth. It will burn up.

☐ Don't pet the horses. They will run wild.

☐ Don't go too far from the earth. It will freeze.

Context Clues: Mighty Hercules

Some people lift weights to build their strength. But Hercules (Her-cu-lees) had a different idea. He carried a calf on his shoulders every day. As the calf grew, it got heavier, and Hercules got stronger. Eventually, Hercules could carry a full-grown bull!

Hercules used his enormous strength to do many kind things. He became famous. Even the king had heard of Hercules! He called for Hercules to kill a lion that had killed many people in his kingdom. Hercules tracked the lion to its den and strangled it. Then Hercules made clothes for himself from the lion's skin. This kind of apparel was unusual, and soon Hercules was recognized everywhere he went. Hercules was big and his clothes made it easy to pick him out in a crowd!

The king asked Hercules to stay in his kingdom and help protect the people who lived there. Hercules performed many feats of strength and bravery. He caught a golden deer for the king. The deer had outrun everyone else. Then Hercules killed a giant, a dragon and other dangerous creatures. Hercules became a hero and was known throughout the kingdom.

Directions: Answer these questions about Hercules.

1. Use context clues to choose the correct definition of **enormous**.

☐ huge   ☐ tiny   ☐ smart

2. Use context clues to choose the correct definition of **strangle**.

☐ beat   ☐ choke   ☐ tickle

3. Use context clues to choose the correct definition of **den**.

☐ pond   ☐ hutch   ☐ home

4. Use context clues to choose the correct definition of **apparel**.

☐ appearance   ☐ clothing   ☐ personality

5. Use context clues to choose the correct definition of **feat**.

☐ trick   ☐ treat   ☐ act

Comprehension: Ceres and Venus

Remember Ceres? She was like Mother Nature to the ancient Romans.

Ceres made the flowers, plants and trees grow. She made crops come up and rain fall. Ceres was a very important goddess. The ancient Romans depended on her for many things.

Although the gods and goddesses were important, they had faults like ordinary people. They argued with one another. Sometimes they got mad and lost their tempers. This is what happened to Ceres and another goddess named Venus (Veen-us). Venus, who was the goddess of love and beauty, got mad at Ceres. She decided to hurt Ceres by causing Pluto, gloomy god of the underworld, to fall in love with Ceres' daughter, Proserpine (Pro-sur-pin-ay).

To accomplish this, Venus sent her son Cupid to shoot Pluto with his bow and arrow. Venus told Cupid that the man shot by this arrow would then fall in love with the first woman he saw. Venus instructed Cupid to make sure that woman was Ceres' daughter. Cupid waited with his bow and arrow until Pluto drove by Ceres' garden in his chariot. In the garden was Proserpine. Just as Pluto's chariot got near her, Cupid shot his arrow.

Ping! The arrow hit Pluto. It did not hurt, but it did its job well. Pluto fell instantly in love with poor Proserpine, who was quietly planting flowers. Pluto was not a gentleman. He did not even introduce himself! Pluto swooped down and carried Proserpine off in his chariot before she could call for help.

Directions: Answer these questions about Ceres and Venus.

1. With whom was Venus angry? _____

2. How did Venus decide to get even? _____

_____

3. Ceres' daughter's name was

☐ Persperpine. ☐ Prosperline. ☐ Proserpine.

4. Venus' son's name was

☐ Apollo. ☐ Cupid. ☐ Persperpine.

Name: _____

Comprehension: Proserpine and Pluto

Proserpine was terrified in Pluto's palace in the underworld. She missed her mother, Ceres, and would not stop crying.

When Ceres discovered her daughter was missing, she searched the whole Earth looking for her. Of course, she did not find her. Ceres was so unhappy about Proserpine's disappearance that she refused to do her job, which was to make things grow. When Ceres did not work, rain could not fall and crops could not grow. Finally, Ceres went to Jupiter for help.

Jupiter was powerful, but so was Pluto. Jupiter told Ceres he could get Proserpine back from Pluto if she had not eaten any of Pluto's food. As it turned out, Proserpine had eaten something. She had swallowed six seeds from a piece of fruit. Because he felt sorry for the people on Earth who were suffering, Pluto told Jupiter that Proserpine could return temporarily to Ceres so she would cheer up and make crops grow again. But Pluto later came back for Proserpine and forced her to spend six months each year with him in the underworld— one month for each seed she had eaten. Every time she returned to the underworld, Ceres mourned and refused to do her job. This is how the Romans explained the seasons—when Proserpine is on Earth with Ceres, it is spring and summer; when Proserpine goes to the underworld, it is fall and winter.

Directions: Answer these questions about Proserpine and Pluto.

1. What happened to Ceres when Pluto took her daughter? _____

_____

2. Whom did Ceres ask for help to get her daughter back? _____

3. Why did Proserpine have to return to Pluto's underworld? _____

_____

4. How long did Proserpine have to stay in the underworld each time she returned?

_____

Name: _____

Comprehension: Orpheus Saves the Day

Orpheus (Or-fee-us) was a talented Greek musician. Once, by playing beautiful music on his lyre (ly-er), he caused a ship that was stuck in the sand to move into the water. (A lyre is a stringed instrument that looks like a small harp and fits in the musician's lap.) The song was about how wonderful it was to sail upon the sea. The ship itself must have thought the song was wonderful, too, because it slipped into the water and sailed away!

There was a reason the ship understood Orpheus' song. Inside the ship was a piece of wood that a goddess had given to the captain of the ship. The captain's name was Jason. Once, Jason had helped an old woman across a deep river. He later learned that the old woman was a goddess. To thank him, the goddess gave Jason a piece of wood that could talk. She told him to use the wood when he built a new ship. If he ever got stuck while building the ship and did not know what to do, the goddess told Jason to ask the wood.

Several times, Jason and his crew got instructions from the wood. Finally, the ship was finished. It was beautiful and very large. Because it was so big, Jason and his men were unable to move it into the water. They called on Hercules for help, and even he could not make it budge. That's when Orpheus saved the day with his lyre.

Directions: Answer these questions about Orpheus' amazing talent.

1. Who owned the ship that was stuck? _____

2. Where was the ship stuck? _____

3. Why did the ship get stuck? _____

4. A lyre looks like what other instrument?

   ☐ harmonica   ☐ guitar   ☐ harp

5. Who did Jason first ask for help to move the ship?

   ☐ Orpheus   ☐ Hercules   ☐ Jupiter

Name: _____

Recalling Details: Centaurs and Minotaurs

Directions: Read the story below about the strange imaginary creatures in Greek mythology called centaurs and minotaurs. Then complete the puzzle.

Besides the gods, there were other powerful creatures in Greek mythology. Among them were minotaurs and centaurs. A minotaur (min-oh-tar) was half man and half bull. A centaur (sen-tar) was half man and half horse. Centaurs were said to live in the mountains near an area of Greece called Thessaly. Minotaurs were said to live in the underworld.

Across:

3. Centaurs were said to live near this area of Greece.

5. A creature that lived in the underworld

7. Minotaurs lived here.

Down:

1. A creature that is half horse

2. Some creatures in Greek mythology were half beast and half _____.

4. Back end of a centaur

5. Another word for Greek stories

6. Back end of a minotaur

Name: _____

Review

Directions: Read the paragraph below. Then circle the answers to the questions in the word search.

Do you remember how Roman and Greek myths came about? People used myths about gods, goddesses and strange creatures to explain why certain things happened. If no rain fell, it was because Ceres was angry. If someone was hit by lightning, it was because that person had angered Jupiter. If a marriage did not work out, Venus or her son Cupid were to blame. If people were wicked, Pluto must have had a hand in their transgressions.

1. Which god or goddess was responsible if no rain fell? _____

2. Which god or goddess was responsible if someone was hit by lightning?

_____

3. Which god or goddess was responsible if a marriage failed? _____

4. Which god or goddess was responsible if people were wicked? _____

5. Choose the correct definition of **transgressions**.

☐ happiness   ☐ sins   ☐ conditions

V	A	D	C	E	R	E	S
W	P	M	U	L	A	R	I
Q	L	A	P	K	B	C	N
J	U	P	I	T	E	R	S
L	T	K	D	A	J	D	I
Y	O	O	S	U	N	E	V

Name: _____

Review

Directions: Follow the instructions below.

1. Define the following words from this section.

    astronomy: _____

    reins: _____

    lyre: _____

    centaur: _____

    minotaur: _____

    myth: _____

2. Choose two words from above and use each in a sentence.

    1)_____

    2)_____

3. Write a summary of the selection "Mighty Hercules" (page 51).

    _____

    _____

    _____

    _____

4. Complete the sequence of events from the selection "Proserpine and Pluto" (page 53).

    1) Pluto fell in love with Proserpine and kidnapped her in his chariot.

    2) _____

    3) _____

    4) _____

    5) _____

Using Prior Knowledge: Art

Directions: Before reading about art in the following section, answer these questions.

1. Write a short paragraph about a famous artist of your choice.

   _____

   _____

   _____

2. Many artists paint realistic scenes. Other artists paint imaginary scenes. Which do you prefer? Why?

   _____

   _____

3. Although we often think of art as painting and drawing, art also includes sculpture, fabric weavings and metalwork. Are you talented at a particularr type of art? If so, what type? If not, what would you like to learn?

   _____

   _____

   _____

4. Why are art museums important to society?

   _____

   _____

   _____

5. Why do you think some artwork is worth so much money? Would you pay several thousand dollars for a piece of artwork? Why or why not?

   _____

   _____

   _____

Main Idea: Creating Art

No one knows exactly when the first human created the first painting. Crude drawings and paintings on the walls of caves show that humans have probably always expressed themselves through art. These early cave pictures show animals being hunted, people dancing and other events of daily life. The simplicity of the paintings reflect the simple lifestyles of these primitive people.

The subjects of early paintings also help to make another important point. Art is not created out of nothing. The subjects an artist chooses to paint reflect the history, politics and culture of the time and place in which he/she lives. An artist born and raised in New York City, for example, is not likely to paint scenes of the Rocky Mountains. An artist living in the Rockies is not likely to paint pictures of city life.

Of course, not all paintings are realistic. Many artists choose to paint pictures that show their own "inner vision" as opposed to what they see with their eyes. Many religious paintings of earlier centuries look realistic but contain figures of angels. These paintings combine the artist's inner vision of angels with other things, such as church buildings, that can be seen.

Directions: Answer these questions about creating art.

1. Circle the main idea:

   Art was important to primitive people because it showed hunting and dancing scenes, and is still important today.

   Through the ages, artists have created paintings that reflect the culture, history and politics of the times, as well as their own inner visions.

2. Why is an artist living in the Rocky Mountains less likely to paint city scenes?

   _____

   _____

3. In addition to what they see with their eyes, what do some artists' paintings also show?

   _____

   _____

Comprehension: Leonardo da Vinci

Many people believe that Leonardo da Vinci, an Italian artist and inventor who lived from 1452 to 1519, was the most brilliant person ever born. He was certainly a man ahead of his time! Records show that da Vinci loved the earth and was curious about everything on it.

To learn about the human body, he dissected corpses to find out what was inside. In the 15th and 16th centuries, dissecting the dead was against the laws of the Catholic church. Leonardo was a brave man!

He was also an inventor. Leonardo invented a parachute and designed a type of helicopter—5 centuries before airplanes were invented! Another of da Vinci's major talents was painting. You have probably seen a print, or copy, of one of his most famous paintings. It is called *The Last Supper*, and shows Jesus eating his final meal with his disciples. It took da Vinci 3 years to paint *The Last Supper*. The man who hired da Vinci to do the painting was upset. He went to da Vinci to ask why it was taking so long. The problem, said da Vinci, was that in the painting, Jesus has just told the disciples that one of them would betray him. He wanted to get their expressions exactly right as each cried out, "Lord, am I the one?"

Another famous painting by da Vinci is called the *Mona Lisa*. Have you seen a print of this painting? Maybe you have been lucky enough to see the original hanging in a Paris art museum called the Louvre (Loov). If so, you know that Mona Lisa has a wistful expression on her face. The painting is a real woman, the wife of an Italian merchant. Art historians believe she looks wistful because one of her children had recently died.

Directions: Answer these questions about Leonardo da Vinci.

1. How old was da Vinci when he died? _____

2. Name two of da Vinci's inventions. _____

3. Name two famous paintings by da Vinci. _____

4. In which Paris museum does *Mona Lisa* hang? ☐ Lourre   ☐ Loure   ☐ Louvre

Context Clues: Leonardo da Vinci

Directions: Read the sentences below. Use context clues to figure out the meaning of the bold words.

1. Some people are **perplexed** when they look at *The Last Supper*, but others understand it immediately.

   ☐ unhappy ☐ happy ☐ puzzled

2. Because his model felt **melancholy** about the death of her child, da Vinci had music played to lift her spirits as he painted the *Mona Lisa*.

   ☐ sad ☐ unfriendly ☐ hostile

3. Because da Vinci's work is so famous, many people **erroneously** assume that he left behind many paintings. In fact, he left only 20.

   ☐ rightly ☐ correctly ☐ wrongly

4. Leonardo da Vinci was not like most other people. He didn't care what others thought of him—he led an interesting and **unconventional** life.

   ☐ dull ☐ not ordinary ☐ ordinary

5. The **composition** of *The Last Supper* is superb. All the parts of the painting seem to fit together beautifully.

   ☐ the picture frame ☐ parts of the picture

6. Leonardo's **genius** set him apart from people with ordinary minds. He never married, he had few friends and he spent much of his time alone.

   ☐ great mental abilities ☐ great physical abilities
   ☐ improper way to do things ☐ proper way to do things

7. Because he was a loner, da Vinci worried no one would come to his funeral when he died. In his will, he set aside 70 cents each to hire 60 **mourners** to accompany his body to his grave.

   ☐ friends ☐ people who grieve ☐ people who smile

Name: _____

Comprehension: Michelangelo

Another famous painter of the late 14th and early 15th centuries was Michelangelo Buonarroti. Michelangelo, who lived from 1475 to 1564, was also an Italian. Like da Vinci, his genius was apparent at a young age. When he was 13, the ruler of his hometown of Florence, Lorenzo Medici (Muh-dee-chee), befriended Michelangelo and asked him to live in the palace. There Michelangelo studied sculpture and met many artists.

By the time he was 18, Michelangelo was a respected sculptor. He created one of his most famous religious sculptures, the *Pieta* (pee-ay-tah), when he was only 21. Then the Medici family abruptly fell from power and Michelangelo had to leave Florence.

Still, his work was well known and he was able to make a living. In 1503, Pope Julius II called Michelangelo to Rome. He wanted Michelangelo to paint the tomb where he would someday be buried. Michelangelo preferred sculpting to painting, but no one turned down the pope! Before Michelangelo finished his painting, however, the pope ordered Michelangelo to begin painting the ceiling of the Sistine Chapel inside the Vatican. (The Vatican is the palace and surrounding area where the pope lives in Rome.)

Michelangelo was very angry! He did not like to paint. He wanted to create sculptures. But no one turns down the pope. After much complaining, Michelangelo began work on what would be his most famous project.

Directions: Answer these questions about Michelangelo.

1. How old was Michelangelo when he died? _____

2. What was the first project Pope Julius II asked Michelangelo to paint?

_____

3. What is the Vatican? _____

4. What was the second project the pope asked Michelangelo to do?

☐ paint his tomb's ceiling   ☐ paint the Sistine Chapel's ceiling

Recalling Details: Michelangelo Puzzler

Directions: Use the facts you learned about Michelangelo to complete the puzzle.

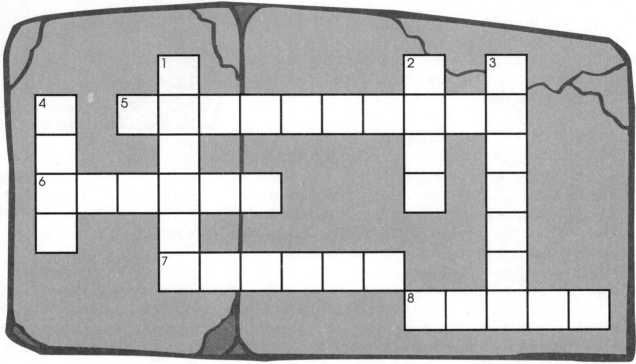

Across:

5. Michelangelo's last name

6. Name of the family who asked Michelangelo to live in the palace

7. Michelangelo like to ____ more than paint.

8. The religious sculpture he created at age 21

Down:

1. The name of the pope who asked Michelangelo to paint

2. The first thing the pope asked Michelangelo to paint

3. The name of the chapel in the Vatican

4. The city in which the Vatican is located

Comprehension: Rembrandt

Most art critics agree that Rembrandt (Rem-brant) was one of the greatest painters of all time. This Dutch artist, who lived from 1606 to 1669, painted some of the world's finest portraits.

Rembrandt, whose full name was Rembrandt van Rijn, was born in Holland to a wealthy family. He was sent to a fine university, but he did not like his studies. He only wanted to paint. He sketched the faces of people around him. During his lifetime, Rembrandt painted 11 portraits of his father and nearly as many of his mother. From the beginning, the faces of old people fascinated him.

When he was 25, Rembrandt went to paint in Amsterdam, a large city in Holland where he lived for the rest of his life. There he married a wealthy woman named Saskia, whom he loved deeply. She died from a disease called tuberculosis (ta-bur-ku-lo-sis) after only 8 years, leaving behind a young son named Titus (Ty-tuss).

Rembrandt was heartbroken over his wife's death. He began to spend all his time painting. But instead of painting what his customers wanted, he painted exactly the way he wanted. Unsold pictures filled his house. They were wonderful paintings, but they were not the type of portraits people wanted. Rembrandt could not pay his debts. He and his son were thrown into the streets. The creditors took his home, his possessions and his paintings. One of the finest painters on Earth was treated like a criminal.

Directions: Answer these questions about Rembrandt.

1. How old was Rembrandt when he died? _____

2. In what city did he spend most of his life? _____

3. How many children did Rembrandt have? _____

4. Rembrandt's wife was named

☐ Sasha.   ☐ Saskia.   ☐ Saksia.

5. These filled his house after his wife's death.

☐ friends   ☐ customers   ☐ unsold paintings

Name: _____

Recalling Details: Rembrandt Puzzler

Directions: Use the facts you learned about Rembrandt to complete the puzzle.

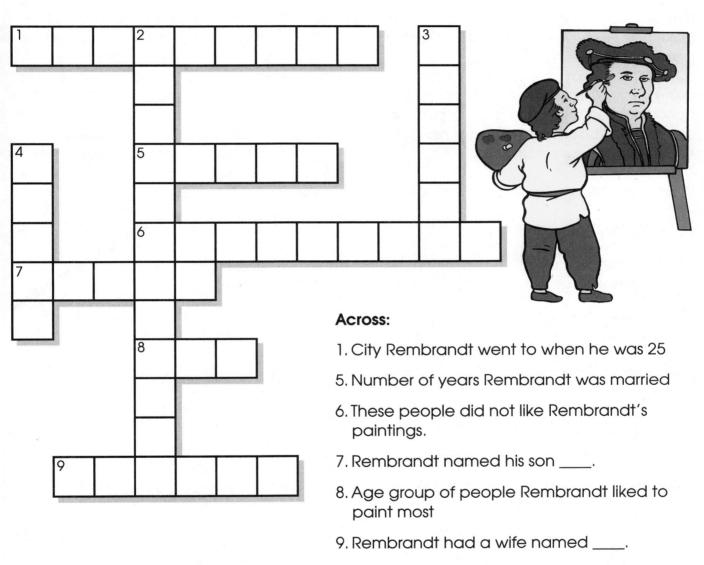

Across:

1. City Rembrandt went to when he was 25

5. Number of years Rembrandt was married

6. These people did not like Rembrandt's paintings.

7. Rembrandt named his son _____.

8. Age group of people Rembrandt liked to paint most

9. Rembrandt had a wife named _____.

Down:

2. The disease from which Rembrandt's wife died

3. Man Rembrandt painted in 11 portraits

4. Rembrandt was thrown out of his house because he could not pay these.

© 1999 American Education Publishing Co.

Comprehension: More About Rembrandt

The people who took Rembrandt's home and possessions left behind something very important. They left his blank canvases and art tools. Also, his housekeeper had hidden a few of his paintings. After he was thrown out of his home, Rembrandt was able to sell the paintings. He moved to a poor neighborhood with his son and housekeeper and began painting again.

For the rest of his life, Rembrandt painted dark paintings. The colors he used included grays, browns and blacks, with a rich yellow color used for contrast. Rembrandt could use dark colors better than any other painter. He painted 145 religious pictures and 650 drawings of subjects from the Bible. If you have ever seen a painting or sketch by Rembrandt, you know that his work seems to portray not just people's faces but their souls as well.

Directions: Answer these questions about Rembrandt.

1. Circle the main idea:

   Rembrandt was not defeated when his home and possessions were taken from him. He continued to paint extraordinary pictures.

   Rembrandt had an unfortunate life and he never got over the treatment he received at the hands of his creditors.

2. Explain how to identify Rembrandt's paintings through the colors he used.

   _____

   _____

3. Choose the correct definition of **sketch**.

   ☐ cartoon   ☐ drawing   ☐ poem

4. How many religious paintings and drawings from the Bible did Rembrandt create?

   _____

5. What is remarkable about Rembrandt's portraits? _____

   _____

Name: _____

Review

Directions: Follow the instructions below.

1. Write a one-sentence main idea for the selection "Leonardo da Vinci" (page 60).

_____

_____

2. Write a summary of the selection "Leonardo da Vinci" (page 60).

_____

_____

_____

3. Complete the sequence of events from the selection "Michelangelo" (page 62).

   1) Michelangelo was born in 1475 in Italy.

   2) _____

   3) _____

   4) _____

   5) _____

   6) _____

   7) _____

4. Define the following words from this section.

   crude: _____

   dissect: _____

   disciples: _____

   merchant: _____

   wistful: _____

Name: _____

Using Prior Knowledge: Stamp Collecting

Directions: Before reading about stamp collecting in the following section, answer these questions.

1. Why do you think people collect stamps?

_____

_____

_____

2. What hobby do you most enjoy? Why?

_____

_____

_____

3. Name at least six famous people who have been pictured on a stamp.

_____ _____

_____ _____

_____ _____

4. Why do you think the postal service issues many different stamps each year? Why not just issue one stamp?

_____

_____

_____

5. The postal service recently introduced self-stick stamps. What are the benefits of these stamps? Do you think these create any drawbacks for collectors?

_____

_____

_____

Name: _____

Fact or Opinion?

Directions: Read the paragraphs below. Then, in the corresponding numbered blanks, write whether each numbered sentence is a fact or an opinion.

(1) An important rule for stamp collectors to follow is never to handle stamps with their fingers. (2) Instead, to keep the stamps clean, collectors use stamp tongs to pick up stamps. (3) Stamps are stored by being placed on mounts. (4) Stamp mounts are plastic holders that fit around the stamp and keep it clean. (5) The backs of the mounts are sticky, so they can be stuck onto a stamp album page. (6) What a great idea!

(7) The stamps are mounted in stamp albums that have either white or black pages. (8) Some people prefer black pages, claiming that the stamps "show" better. (9) Some people prefer white pages, claiming that they give the album a cleaner look. (10) I think this foolish bickering over page colors is ridiculous!

1. _____

2. _____

3. _____

4. _____

5. _____

6. _____

7. _____

8. _____

9. _____

10. _____

© 1999 American Education Publishing Co.

Name: _____

Comprehension: More Stamp Collecting

Many people collect stamps in blocks of four. Each stamp in the block is stuck to the other stamps along the edges. Collectors do not tear the stamps apart from one another. They buy blocks of stamps bearing new designs directly from the post office. Then they mount the blocks of stamps and place them in their albums.

Collectors also get their stamps off of envelopes. This is a bit tricky, because the stamps are glued on. Usually, collectors soak the stamps in warm water to loosen the glue. Then they gently pull the stamps from the paper and let them dry before mounting them.

Some beginners start their collections by buying a packet of mixed stamps. The packets, or bags, contain a variety of different stamps. Beginners buy these packets from companies that supply stamps to philatelists (fuh-lay-tell-lists). Philately (fuh-lay-tell-lee) is the collection and study of postage stamps. Philatelists are the people who collect and study them.

Packets of stamps usually contain stamps from many different countries. Often, they contain duplicates of some of the stamps. Suppliers usually don't sort the stamps that go into the packets for beginners. They leave that for beginning philatelists to enjoy!

Directions: Answer these questions about stamp collecting.

1. Name three places some people get stamps. _____

_____

2. What is the word that describes the collection and study of stamps? _____

3. What are people called who collect and study stamps? _____

4. The bag that a mixture of stamps comes in is called a

☐ postal bag.　　☐ packet.　　☐ philatelist.

5. Do stamp mixtures usually include only U.S. stamps?

☐ Yes　　　　☐ No

Recalling Details: Philately Abbreviations

Like other hobbies, philately has its own jargon and symbols. Collectors and dealers know what they mean, but "outsiders" would be puzzled if they saw the following abbreviations without their definitions. Read them carefully, then refer to them when answering the questions below.

Avg. — average condition

blk. — block of four stamps

C — cancelled (used) stamp

OG — original gum

       (glue on back of stamp)

G — good condition

M — mint (excellent and unused) condition

s — single stamp

U — used stamp

VF — very fine condition

Wmk — watermark (can occur when water

       is used to remove stamp from envelope)

Directions: Answer these questions about the abbreviations used by stamp dealers and collectors.

1. If a philatelist wrote the following description, what would he/she mean?

   I have a blk. in VF. _____

   _____

2. What does this mean? **s with OG, condition M** _____

   _____

3. What other abbreviation would most likely be used do describe a used (U) stamp?

   _____

4. What does this mean? **s in Avg. with Wmk** _____

   _____

5. Which is more valuable, a rare stamp in **M** or **VF** condition? _____

6. Would you rather own a single U stamp or a blk. in M? _____

Comprehension: Faces on Stamps

If anyone ever tries to sell you a stamp with a picture of former Vice President Dan Quayle on it, just say no! In the United States, only people who have died can have their pictures on stamps. That is why the singer Elvis Presley's face appeared on stamps only after he died.

Many U.S. presidents' faces have been on postage stamps, as have pictures of the faces of other important people in U.S. history. Some people's faces have been on many different stamps. Through the years, George Washington and Benjamin Franklin have been on dozens of different types of stamps!

Other people whose pictures have been on stamps include John Quincy Adams, the sixth president of the United States; Jane Addams, a U.S. social worker and writer; Louisa May Alcott, author of *Little Women* and many other books; Clara Barton, nurse and founder of the American Red Cross; Alexander Graham Bell, inventor of the telephone; and poet, Emily Dickinson. These are only a few of the hundreds of famous Americans whose faces have appeared on U.S. postage stamps.

Directions: Answer these questions about some of the people whose faces have appeared on U.S. stamps.

1. Name six occupations of people whose faces have appeared on postage stamps.

_____

_____

2. What two people's pictures have appeared on more stamps than on any others?

_____

3. Why can't Dan Quayle's face appear on a postage stamp? _____

_____

4. Which person featured on a postage stamp was a social worker?

☐ Clara Barton   ☐ Louisa May Alcott   ☐ Jane Addams

5. Which person featured on a postage stamp was an inventor?

☐ Emily Dickinson   ☐ Alexander Graham Bell   ☐ John Quincy Adams

Name: _____

Recalling Details: Postage Stamp Puzzler

Directions: Use the facts you learned about the faces on postage stamps to complete the puzzle. (There is no space between answers that have more than two words.)

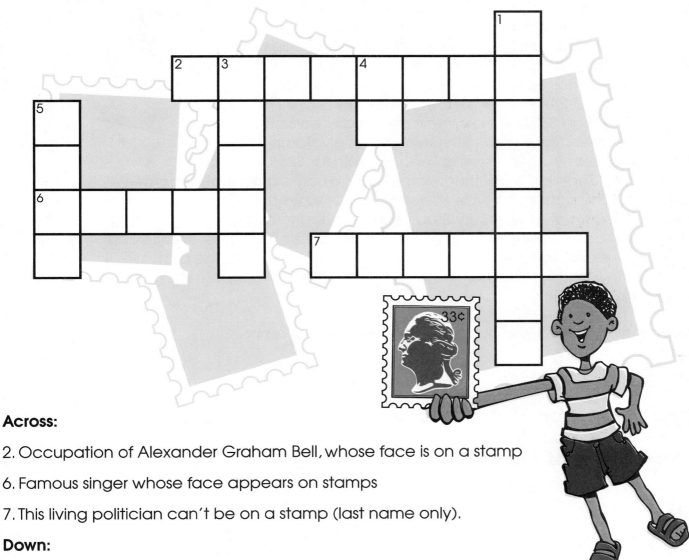

Across:

2. Occupation of Alexander Graham Bell, whose face is on a stamp

6. Famous singer whose face appears on stamps

7. This living politician can't be on a stamp (last name only).

Down:

1. Along with Washington, he's appeared on the most stamps.

3. Occupation of Clara Barton, whose face is on a stamp

4. Can President Clinton be on a stamp?

5. Occupation of Emily Dickinson, whose face is on a stamp

Comprehension: Valuable Stamps

Most people collect stamps as a hobby. They spend small sums of money to get the stamps they want, or they trade stamps with other collectors. They rarely make what could be considered "big money" from their philately hobby.

A few collectors are in the business of philately as opposed to the hobby. To the people who can afford it, some stamps are worth big money. For example, a U.S. airmail stamp with a face value of 24 cents when it was issued in 1918 is now worth more than $35,000 if a certain design appears on the stamp. Another stamp, the British Guiana, an ugly stamp that cost only a penny when it was issued, later sold for $280,000!

The Graf Zeppelin is another example of an ugly stamp that became valuable. Graf Zeppelin is the name of a type of airship, similar to what we now call a "blimp," invented around the turn of the century. Stamps were issued to mark the first roundtrip flight the *Zeppelin* made between two continents. A set of three of these stamps cost $4.55 when they were issued. The stamps were ugly and few of them sold. The postal service destroyed the rest. Now, because they are rare, each set of the Graf Zeppelin stamps is worth hundreds of dollars.

Directions: Answer these questions about valuable stamps.

1. What is the most valuable stamp described? _____

2. For how much did this stamp originally sell? _____

3. What did a collector later pay for it? _____

4. The Graf Zeppelin stamps originally sold for $4.55 for a set of

☐ four.   ☐ six.   ☐ three.

5. Which stamp did the postal service destroy because it didn't sell?

☐ British Guiana   ☐ Graf Zeppelin   ☐ British Zeppelin

Name: _____

Fact or Opinion?

Directions: Read the paragraphs below. Then, in the corresponding numbered blanks, write whether each numbered sentence is a fact or an opinion.

(1) Nearly every valuable stamp on Earth has been counterfeited (coun-ter-fit-tid) at one time or another. (2) A "counterfeit" is a fake that looks nearly identical to the original. (3) It takes a lot of nerve to try to pass off counterfeits as the real thing. (4) Counterfeiting is big business, especially with stamps from overseas. (5) Because a collector often has no original for comparison, he/she can be easily fooled by a good counterfeit!

(6) One way people can make sure a stamp is real is to have it checked by a company that authenticates (aw-then-ti-kates) stamps. (7) To "authenticate" means to prove the stamp is real. (8) Of course, there is a fee for this service. (9) But I think paying a reasonable fee is worth what collectors get in return. (10) Those counterfeiters should be locked up forever!

1. _____

2. _____

3. _____

4. _____

5. _____

6. _____

7. _____

8. _____

9. _____

10. _____

Comprehension: Stamp Value

It's nearly impossible to predict which stamps will rise in value. Why? Because the value is based on the law of supply and demand. How much does someone or a group of "someones" want for a particular stamp? If many people want a stamp, the value will increase, especially if few of the stamps exist.

However, collectors are also always on the lookout for things that can lower the value of a stamp. Are the stamp's perforations (per-four-ay-shuns) torn along the edges? (Perforations are ragged edges where stamps tear apart.) Is there a watermark on the stamp? Has the gum worn off the back? All these things can make a stamp less valuable.

Directions: Answer these questions about determining the value of stamps.

1. Name three things that can lower the value of a stamp.

_____

_____

2. Collecting stamps is a fascinating hobby.   Fact   Opinion

3. What is one thing the value of stamps is based upon? _____

4. What will happen if many people want a rare stamp?_____

_____

5. Explain how to spot a stamp that will become valuable. _____

_____

_____

_____

Name: _____

Review

Directions: Follow the instructions below.

1. Define the following words from this section.

mount: _____

bickering: _____

philately: _____

counterfeit: _____

authenticate: _____

perforations: _____

2. Choose two of the words above and use each in a sentence.

1)_____

2)_____

3. Write a one-sentence main idea for the selection "Stamp Value" (page 76).

_____

_____

4. Write a summary of the selection "Faces on Stamps" (page 72).

_____

_____

_____

5. Write a summary of the selection "More About Stamp Collecting" (page 70).

_____

_____

_____

© 1999 American Education Publishing Co.

Name: _____

Using Prior Knowledge: Writing

Directions: Before reading about writing in the following section, answer these questions.

1. What are some of the benefits of writing for young people?

_____

_____

_____

2. What are some of the disadvantages of writing for young people?

_____

_____

_____

3. What type of writing do you most enjoy? Why?

_____

_____

_____

4. Why might it be difficult for a young person your age to publish his/her work?

_____

_____

_____

5. On another sheet of paper, write a short journal entry describing how you feel about writing. Discuss whether you enjoy writing poetry, fiction, nonfiction, letters, and so on; if you find writing difficult or easy; and when and where you feel most comfortable writing.

Name: _____

Comprehension: Calling Young Poets and Writers!

Do you like to write poetry, short stories or articles? If so, you will be glad to learn that there are magazines dedicated to publishing children's writing.

Shoe Tree is a magazine for children ages 6 to 14. It's published three times a year by the National Association for Young Writers. Fictional stories, articles, poems, book reviews and humorous essays are all published in *Shoe Tree*. The magazine is headquartered at 215 Valle del Sol Drive, Santa Fe, New Mexico 87501.

Another magazine that publishes children's writing is *Stone Soup*. *Stone Soup* is published by the Children's Art Foundation, Box 83, Santa Cruz, California 95063. *Stone Soup* publishes poetry, science fiction, fiction and personal experience essays. This magazine also publishes drawings by children. *Stone Soup* publishes the work of children up to age 13.

A literary journal for young people is *Writes of Passage: The Literary Journal for Teenagers.* *Writes of Passage* is published by Writes of Passage USA, Inc., P.O. Box 1935, Livingston, New Jersey 07039. *Writes of Passage* accepts poems and short stories written by teens between 12 and 19.

Like all professional publications, *Shoe Tree, Stone Soup* and *Writes of Passage* want work that is spelled and punctuated correctly. Typed papers are preferred, but *Shoe Tree* will accept handwritten stories and poems that are clearly readable.

Directions: Answer these questions about magazines that publish children's writing.

1. In which publication can 15 year olds be published? _____

2. If you are 14, you are too old to write for which magazine? _____

3. Which publication is published in Santa Fe? _____

4. Which publication will accept handwritten stories?

☐ *Shoe Tree*   ☐ *Stone Soup*   ☐ *Writes of Passage*

Name: _____

Comprehension: Poems for Kids of All Ages

You're never too young or too old to appreciate poetry! Each year, many books of poems are published for children of all ages. The following books were published in 1990.

Nursery Poems and Prayers and *Nursery Songs and Lullabies* are books for very young children. Older kids will enjoy reading these books, also. You may remember a parent reading some of these poems to you when you were a small child. The author of both books is Bessie Pease Gutmann. The books are published by a company called Grosset & Dunlap.

If you like silly poems and riddles, you may enjoy *My Head Is Red and Other Riddle Rhymes*. The author is Myra Cohn Livingston. The publisher is Holiday House. The book contains 27 riddle poems for children ages 6 to 9.

A book of poems for children age 12 and older is *Life Doesn't Frighten Me at All*. The poems were compiled by John Agard. "Compiled by" means that Mr. Agard collected the poems from other places. He did not write the poems himself. The poems in *Life Doesn't Frighten Me at All* are about growing up, families and politics. The publisher is Henry Holt.

Directions: Answer these questions about the four poetry books.

1. What company published *Nursery Songs and Lullabies*? _____

2. Who is the author of *Nursery Poems and Prayers*?

_____

3. Who is the author of *My Head Is Red and Other Riddle Rhymes*?

_____

4. Which book is for children age 12 and older?_____

5. Who complied the poems in *Life Doesn't Frighten Me at All*? _____

6. Which book is for children ages 6 to 9?_____

_____

7. Where were all these books published?_____

_____

Comprehension: *Highlights for Children*

Young writers today are lucky to have many magazines interested in publishing their work. Just as farmers take pigs and cows to markets to sell them, writers also have markets. Writers' markets are the magazines and newspapers that publish the things they write.

An excellent market for children's writing is *Highlights for Children. Highlights* is published at 803 Church Street, Honesdale, Pennsylvania 18431. A young writer who is published in this magazine will have many people read his/her work. *Highlights* has a circulation of more than 2 million! This means more than 2 million copies are printed and mailed each month to people who pay to receive it. Those people are called "subscribers."

About 20 percent of *Highlights* is written by children. Young writers up to age 15 can submit poetry, articles, jokes, riddles and pictures. Besides these opportunities for young writers, *Highlights* sponsors a fiction contest each year. Stories for the fiction contest should be no longer than 900 words. The type of fiction young writers are invited to submit changes each year.

In 1990, for example, *Highlights* editors asked young writers to send them humorous fiction. The deadline for the fiction contest is usually very early in the year. A "deadline" is the date by which a writer's work must be received by the publisher. Writing submitted after a deadline will not be considered for publication. Information about the annual fiction contest is printed in the fall issue of *Highlights*.

Directions: Answer these questions about *Highlights* magazine.

1. What are writers' markets? _____

_____

2. What does "circulation" mean? _____

_____

3. What is a subscriber? _____

4. *Highlights* is published in

☐ New York City.   ☐ Honesdale, Pennsylvania.

5. *Highlights* accepts writing from children up to age

☐ 13.   ☐ 14.   ☐ 15.

Sequencing: Studying the Market

The writing of many talented young authors is often rejected because they send their work to the wrong type of magazine. For example, a beautiful poem sent to the editor of a magazine that publishes only science fiction is bound to be rejected. "Rejecting" a piece of writing means the editor does not want to print it in the magazine.

A sensible way to cut down the number of times a piece of writing is rejected is to first study the market. Remember, writers' markets are the magazines and newspapers that publish the things they write. "Studying" a particular market simply means that you should carefully read a copy of the magazine you would like to be published in.

Knowing the type of writing a magazine publishes will help you "target" your market. "Targeting" simply means picking out a magazine that publishes your type of writing. If you study the markets, then target them, you will send your beautiful poem only to magazines that publish poetry.

It is a good idea to check your work to see if it meets the needs of the magazines you have targeted. Is it too long or too short compared to other poems or stories printed in the magazine? Is the content too difficult or too easy? Revise your writing, if necessary. Then write a short letter to the editor, telling briefly about what you have written. Remember to include your home address and phone number! In a large envelope, put what you have written, the letter, and a self-addressed, stamped envelope for the editor's reply.

Directions: Number in order the steps to take before submitting a piece of writing to an editor.

_____ Mail what you have written to the editor.

_____ Get several magazines for young writers.

_____ Write a short letter to the editor about your work.

_____ Target the magazines that might publish your type of writing.

_____ Study the magazines to find out the type of writing they publish.

_____ Check and revise your piece of writing, if necessary.

_____ Include a stamped, self-addressed envelope with your writing.

Comprehension: "The Trains"

In the evening from my window

Just before I go to bed,

I can watch the trains a-gliding

As the stars shine overhead.

How I wonder where they're going,

What they'll see upon their rounds—

Mighty mountains, lonely forests,

Sleeping cities, silent towns.

Directions: Answer these questions about "The Trains."

1. Who is watching the trains? _____

2. From what room do you think the speaker is watching? _____

3. When is the speaker observing the trains? _____

4. Where does the speaker think the trains are going? _____

_____

5. How does the speaker say the trains move? _____

6. Why do you think the speaker likes to watch trains? _____

_____

Name: _____

Comprehension/Sequencing: Limericks

Limericks (lim-riks) are five-line poems that tend to be silly. The last word in certain lines of a limerick rhyme with the last word in other lines. This is called the poem's rhyme scheme. Usually, each line of a limerick has five to eight syllables. Here is a silly limerick. Can you use it as an example to write a limerick of your own?

There once was a girl from Hong Kong

Whose hair was abnormally long.

When she sat on the couch,

She always yelled, "Ouch!"

Then screamed that her hair was all wrong!

Directions: Answer these questions about limericks.

1. Which lines rhyme in the rhyme scheme of the limerick above?

_____

2. Number in order the events in the limerick.

_____ The girl screamed that her hair was all wrong.

_____ The girl grew her hair too long.

_____ The girl yelled, "Ouch!"

_____ The girl sat on the couch.

3. How many syllables does line one in the limerick have? _____

4. How many syllables does line three in the limerick have? _____

5. Why is the girl's hair "all wrong"? _____

6. What does "rhyme scheme" mean? _____

_____

Review

Directions: Follow the instructions below.

1. Summarize the message of the poem "The Trains."

_____

_____

_____

2. List four publications that publish young people's work.

_____   _____

_____   _____

3. Why is it important to revise and edit your work several times?

_____

_____

4. Write a one-sentence main idea for the selection "*Highlights for Children*" (page 81).

_____

_____

5. Write a summary of the selection "Studying the Market" (page 82).

_____

_____

_____

6. Write a silly limerick of your own below.

_____

_____

_____

Using Prior Knowledge: Big Cats

Directions: Before reading about big cats in the following section, answer these questions.

1. Name at least four big wild cats.

_____   _____

_____   _____

2. Compare and contrast a house cat with a wild cat.

_____

_____

_____

_____

3. What impact might the expansion of human population and housing have on big cats?

_____

_____

_____

4. Do you have a cat? What are the special qualities of this pet? Write about your cat's name and its personality traits. If you don't have a cat, write about a cat you would like to have.

_____

_____

_____

_____

Name: _____

Comprehension: Jaguars

The jaguar is a large cat, standing up to 2 feet tall at the shoulder. Its body can reach 73 inches long, and the tail can be another 30 inches long. The jaguar is characterized by its yellowish-red coat covered with black spots. The spots themselves are made up of a central spot surrounded by a circle of spots.

Jaguars are not known to attack humans, but some ranchers claim that jaguars attack their cattle. This claim has given jaguars a bad reputation.

The jaguar can be found in southern North America, but is most populous in Central and South America. Jaguars are capable climbers and swimmers, and they eat a wide range of animals.

Female jaguars have between one and four cubs after a gestation of 93 to 105 days. Cubs stay with the mother for 2 years. Jaguars are known to have a life expectancy of at least 22 years.

Directions: Use context clues for these definitions.

1. populous: _____

2. reputation: _____

3. gestation: _____

Directions: Answer these questions about jaguars.

4. Describe the spots on a jaguar's coat.

_____

_____

5. Why would it be to a jaguar's advantage to have spots on its coat?

_____

_____

Comprehension: Leopards

The leopard is a talented nocturnal hunter and can see very well in the dark. Because of its excellent climbing ability, the leopard is able to stalk and kill monkeys and baboons. Leopards are also known to consume mice, porcupines and fruit. Although the true leopard is characterized by a light beige coat with black spots, some leopards can be entirely black. These leopards are called black panthers. Many people refer to other cat species as leopards. Cheetahs are sometimes referred to as hunting leopards. The clouded leopard lives in southeastern Asia and has a grayish spotted coat. The snow leopard, which has a white coat, lives in Central Asia.

LEOPARD

A leopard's spots help to camouflage (cam-o-floj) it as it hunts.

True leopards can grow to over 6 feet long, not including their 3-foot-long tail. Leopards can be found in Africa and Asia.

Directions: Use context clues for these definitions.

1. consume: _____

2. ability: _____

3. nocturnal: _____

Directions: Answer these questions about leopards.

4. List three differences between the leopard and the jaguar.

_____

_____

_____

_____

_____

_____

5. What makes a leopard able to hunt monkeys and baboons?

_____

Comprehension: Lynxes

Lynxes are strange-looking cats with very long legs and large paws. Their bodies are a mere 51 inches in length, and they have short little tails. Most lynxes have a clump of hair that extends past the tip of their ears.

Lynxes not only are known to chase down their prey, but also to leap on them from a perch above the ground. They eat small mammals and birds, as well as an occasional deer.

There are four types of lynxes. Bobcats can be found in all areas of the United States except the Midwest. The Spanish lynx is an endangered species. The Eurasian lynx, also known as the northern lynx, and the Canadian lynx are two other kinds of lynxes.

Directions: Use context clues for these definitions.

1. prey: _____

2. perch: _____

Directions: Answer these questions about lynxes.

3. What are the four types of lynxes? _____

_____

4. Use the following words in a sentence of your own.

mammal _____

endangered _____

5. Do you believe it is important to classify animals as "endangered" to protect a species that is low in population? Explain your answer.

_____

_____

_____

Comprehension: Pumas

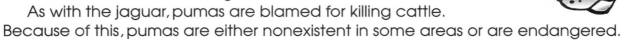

The puma is a cat most recognized by the more popular names of "cougar" or "mountain lion." Just like other large cats, the puma is a carnivore. It feeds on deer, elk and other mammals. It can be found in both North and South America. Pumas have small heads with a single black spot above each eye. The coat color ranges from bluish-gray (North America) to reddish-brown (South America). The underside of the body, as well as the throat and muzzle, are white. The puma's body can be almost 6 feet long, not including the tail.

Female pumas give birth to two to four young. When first born, pumas have brown spots on their backs, and their tails are lined with dark brown rings.

As with the jaguar, pumas are blamed for killing cattle. Because of this, pumas are either nonexistent in some areas or are endangered.

Directions: Answer these questions about pumas.

1. What is a muzzle? _____

2. As the population increases in North America, predict what might happen to pumas.

_____

_____

_____

3. What are two other popular names for the puma? _____

4. What other cat besides the puma is blamed for killing cattle? _____

5. Reviewing the sizes of cats discussed so far, write their names in order, from smallest to largest.

1)_____ 2)_____

3)_____ 4)_____

Comprehension: Cheetahs

The cheetah can be found on the continent of Africa. Small numbers of cheetahs also live in Iran. Because its range has been drastically reduced, the cheetah is now endangered in tropical Africa. Because of its diminishing population and area, cheetahs are inbreeding, which affects genetic variations in the species. These variations can cause weaknesses to arise in the population.

The cheetah has a yellowish-brown coat with black spots. Cheetah's bodies grow to almost 5 feet long. Cheetahs are nearly the same weight as leopards, at about 130 pounds, but they have longer legs and bodies.

Unlike other cats, cheetahs are not capable of retracting their claws. They use their sense of sight rather than smell to hunt. The cheetah is the fastest animal on land. It can reach speeds of 68 miles per hour and, therefore, is able to outrun its prey.

Cheetahs often travel alone. Females only travel in groups when raising their cubs. Male cheetahs travel with females only during mating season.

Directions: Answer these questions about cheetahs.

1. What are the qualities that help a cheetah to hunt?

_____

_____

2. What is the danger to a species when inbreeding takes place?

_____

_____

Directions: Use context clues for these definitions.

3. range: _____

4. diminishing: _____

5. genetic: _____

6. variations: _____

Comprehension: Tigers

Tigers live on the continent of Asia. The tiger is the largest cat, often weighing over 500 pounds. Its body can grow to be 9 feet long and the tail up to 36 inches in length.

There are three types of tigers. The Siberian tiger is very rare and has a yellow coat with dark stripes. The Bengal tiger can be found in southeastern Asian and central India. Its coat is more orange and its stripes are darker. There is a tiger that lives on the island of Sumatra as well. It is smaller and darker in color than the Bengal tiger.

Tigers lead solitary lives. They meet with other tigers only to mate and share food or water. Tigers feed primarily on deer and cattle but are also known to eat fish and frogs. If necessary, tigers will also eat dead animals.

Female tigers bear one to six cubs at a time. The cubs stay with their mother for almost 2 years before going out on their own.

Because tiger parts are in high demand for use in Chinese medicine and recipes, tigers have been hunted almost to extinction. All tigers are currently listed as endangered.

Directions: Use context clues for these definitions.

1. rare: _____

2. solitary: _____

3. extinction: _____

Directions: Answer these questions about tigers.

4. Why have tigers been hunted almost to extinction?

_____

_____

5. Name the three types of tigers.

_____

Comprehension: Lions

The lion, often referred to as the king of beasts, once commanded a large territory. Today, their territory is very limited. Lions are savanna-dwelling animals, which has made them easy targets for hunters. The increasing population of humans and their livestock has also contributed to the lion's decreased population.

Lions are heavy cats. Males weigh over 500 pounds and can grow to be over 8 feet in length, with a tail over 36 inches long. Males are characterized by a long, full mane that covers the neck and most of the head and shoulders. Females do not have a mane and are slightly smaller in size. Both males and females have beige coats, hooked claws and powerful jaws. Their roars can be heard up to 5 miles away!

Lions tend to hunt in the evening and spend the day sleeping. They prefer hunting zebra or giraffe but will eat almost anything. A lion is capable of eating over 75 pounds of meat at a single kill and then go a week without eating again. Generally, female lions do the hunting, and the males come to share the kill.

Lions live in groups called prides. Each pride has between 4 and 37 lions. Females bear one to four cubs approximately every 2 years.

Directions: Answer these questions about lions.

1. What are the differences between male and female lions? _____

_____

2. Why would living on a savanna make the lion an "easy target"? _____

_____

Directions: Use context clues for these definitions.

3. pride: _____

4. territory: _____

5. savanna: _____

6. capable: _____

Recalling Details: Big Cats

Directions: Complete the chart with the information you learned about big cats. You may need reference books or the Internet to help you answer some of these questions.

	Size	Color	# of Young	Food	Location
Jaguar					
Leopard					
Lynx					
Puma					
Cheetah					
Tiger					
Lion					

Review

Directions: Follow the instructions below.

1. Choose any two big cats from this section and compare them.

_____

_____

_____

_____

2. Why are each of these big cats endangered or decreasing in number?

_____

_____

_____

3. What can be done to get these big cats off the endangered list?

_____

_____

_____

4. Now that you have read about big cats, compare and contrast them with a house cat. What do you know now that you didn't know before reading this section?

_____

_____

_____

_____

Using Prior Knowledge: Famous Ships

Directions: Before reading about famous ships in the following section, answer these questions.

1. Look up the following terms in a dictionary and write their definitions.

   vessel: _____

   bow: _____

   stern: _____

   poop deck: _____

   hull: _____

   caravel: _____

   mast: _____

   frigate: _____

   lateen: _____

   spar: _____

   fore: _____

   aft: _____

2. Have you ever been on a large ship? If so, describe the experience. If not, on what kind of ship or boat would you like to ride? Why?

   _____

   _____

   _____

3. Name at least one famous ship and write what you know about it.

   _____

   _____

   _____

Comprehension: The *Constitution*

The *Constitution*, or "Old Ironsides," was built by the United States Navy in 1798. Its success in battle made it one of the most famous vessels in the United States. The Constitution's naval career began with the war with Tripoli from 1803 to 1804. Later, it was also used in the War of 1812. During this war, it was commanded by Isaac Hull. The *Constitution* won a 30-minute battle with the British ship, *Guerriere*, in August of 1812. The *Guerriere* was nearly demolished. Later that same year, the *Constitution* was used to capture a British frigate near Brazil.

The *Constitution* was taken out of service in 1829 and was rebuilt many times over the years. Today, it is on display at the Boston Navy Yard.

Directions: Answer these questions about the *Constitution*.

1. What is the main idea of the selection? _____

_____

2. Which ship was almost demolished by the *Constitution*? _____

3. In which two wars was the *Constitution* used? _____

4. Where is the *Constitution* now on display? _____

5. Complete the following time line with dates and events described above.

_____   _____   _____   _____   _____

⊢————+————————+————————+————————+————————+————————⊣

Comprehension: The *Santa Maria, Niña* and *Pinta*

When Christopher Columbus decided to attempt a voyage across the ocean, the ships he depended upon to take him there were called "caravels." A caravel is a small sailing ship built by Spain and Portugal in the 15th and 16th centuries. The caravels Columbus used to sail to the New World were named Santa Maria, Niña, and Pinta.

The ships were not very large. It is believed the Santa Maria was only 75 to 90 feet long, and the Niña and Pinta were only about 70 feet long. Caravels typically had three to four masts with sails attached. The foremast carried a square sail, while the others were more triangular in shape. These triangular-shaped sails were called "lateen sails."

These three small ships were quite seaworthy and proved excellent ships for Columbus. They got him where he wanted to go.

Directions: Answer these questions about the *Santa Maria, Niña* and *Pinta*.

1. What is a lateen sail? _____

2. What is the main idea of the selection? _____

   _____

   _____

3. What is a caravel? _____

4. Where did Columbus sail in his caravels? _____

5. Do some research and compare a 15th-century caravel with a ship built in the 20th century.

   _____

   _____

   _____

   _____

Comprehension: The *Lusitania*

The *Lusitania* was a British passenger steamship. It became famous when it was torpedoed and sunk by the Germans during World War I. On May 7, 1915, the *Lusitania* was traveling off the coast of Ireland when a German submarine fired on it without warning. The ship stood no chance of surviving the attack and sunk in an astonishing 20 minutes. 1,198 people perished, of whom 128 were American citizens. At the time the ship was torpedoed, the United States was not yet involved in the war. Public opinion over the attack put pressure on President Woodrow Wilson to declare war on Germany. The Germans proclaimed that the *Lusitania* was carrying weapons for the use of the allies.

This claim was later proven to be true. President Wilson demanded that the German government apologize for the sinking and make amends. Germany did not accept responsibility but did promise to avoid sinking any more passenger ships without first giving a warning.

Directions: Answer these questions about the *Lusitania*.

1. What does **proclaimed** mean? _____

2. What does **perished** mean? _____

3. What does **amends** mean? _____

4. What does **allies** mean? _____

5. If the *Lusitania* was carrying arms, do you think the Germans had a right to sink it? Why or why not?

_____

_____

_____

_____

Comprehension: The *Titanic*

The British passenger ship, *Titanic*, debuted in the spring of 1912. It was billed as an unsinkable ship due to its construction. It had 16 watertight compartments that would hold the ship afloat even in the event that four of the compartments were damaged.

But on the evening of April 14, 1912, during *Titanic's* first voyage, its design proved unworthy. Just before midnight, *Titanic* struck an iceberg, which punctured 5 of the 16 compartments. The ship sunk in a little under 3 hours. Approximately 1,513 of the over 2,220 people onboard died.

Most of these people died because there weren't enough lifeboats to accommodate everyone onboard. These people were left floating in the water. Many died from exposure, since the Atlantic Ocean was near freezing in temperature. It was one of the worst ocean disasters in history.

Because of the investigations that followed the *Titanic* disaster, the passenger ship industry instituted many reforms. It is now required that there is ample lifeboat space for all passengers and crew. An international ice patrol and full-time radio coverage were also instituted to prevent such disasters in the future.

Directions: Answer these questions about the *Titanic*.

1. How did most of the 1,513 people on board the *Titanic* die? _____

2. Why did this "unsinkable" ship sink? _____

   _____

3. What changes have been made in ship safety as a result of the *Titanic* tragedy?

   _____

   _____

4. There have been many attempts to rescue artifacts from the *Titanic*. But many families of the dead wish the site to be left alone, as it is the final resting place of their relatives. They feel burial sites should not be disrupted. Do you agree or disagree? Why?

   _____

   _____

   _____

Venn Diagram: *Lusitania* and *Titanic*

A **Venn diagram** is used to chart information that shows similarities and differences between two things.

Example:

Dogs	Both	Cats
barks	good pet	one size
dependent	can live inside or outside	kills mice
large and small breeds	has fur	can use litterbox
protects the home	four legs	independent

Directions: Complete the Venn diagram for the *Lusitania* and the *Titanic*.

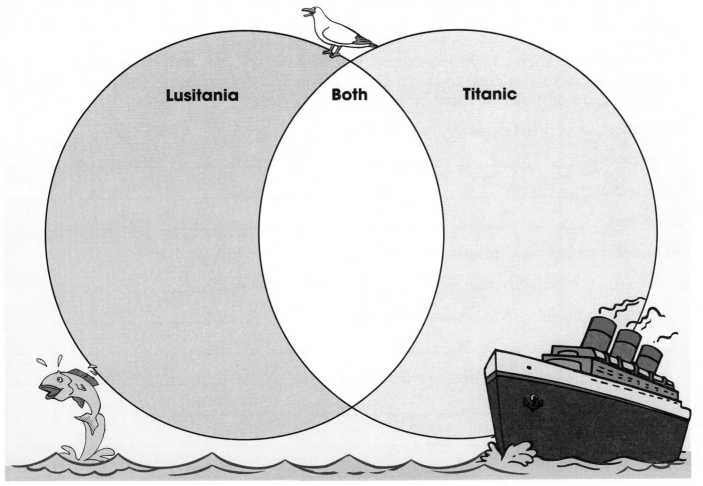

Lusitania   Both   Titanic

Name: _____

Comprehension: The *Monitor* and the *Virginia*

During the Civil War, it became customary to cover wooden warships with iron. This increased their durability and made them more difficult to sink. Two such ships were built using iron. They were the *Monitor* and the *Virginia*.

Most people are more familiar with the name the *Merrimack*. The *Merrimack* was a U.S. steam frigate that had been burnt and sunk by Union forces when the Confederates were forced to abandon their navy yard. The Confederate Navy raised the hull of the *Merrimack* and rebuilt her as the ironclad *Virginia*.

Both the *Monitor* and the *Virginia* engaged in battle on March 9, 1962. After several hours of battle, the bulky *Virginia* had no choice but to withdraw in order to avoid the lowering tides. This battle, called Hampton Roads, was considered to be a tie between the two ships.

Although both ships survived the battle, they were later destroyed. Two months later, the *Virginia* was sunk by her crew to avoid capture. The *Monitor* was sunk on December 31, 1862, during a storm off the coast of North Carolina.

Directions: Use context clues for these definitions.

1. customary: _____

2. durability: _____

3. ironclad: _____

Directions: Answer these questions about the *Monitor* and the *Virginia*.

4. Who won the battle between the *Virginia* and the *Monitor*? _____

5. Why would lowering tides present danger to a ship? _____

_____

6. Describe how each ship was finally destroyed. _____

_____

_____

_____

_____

Review

1. Use the Venn diagram you completed comparing the *Lusitania* and the *Titanic* (page 101) to write a two-paragraph compare/contrast essay about the two ships. Describe their similarities in the first paragraph and their differences in the second.

_____

_____

_____

_____

_____

_____

_____

_____

2. Describe the differences in the structure of the following ships: *Santa Maria, Monitor* and *Titanic*.

_____

_____

_____

_____

3. Why did people think the *Titanic* was unsinkable? After the ship actually did sink, how do you think this affected the way people thought about new technology?

_____

_____

_____

_____

_____

Cumulative Review

Directions: Follow the instructions below.

1. Write a paragraph comparing folk music and jazz music.

_____

_____

_____

_____

2. Complete the following chart with information from the section about farm animals.

	Pigs	Cows	Sheep	Goats
Gestation period (if known)				
Number of young for each pregnancy				
Human uses for this animal				
Interesting fact about the animal				

3. Write a description of each type of book.

legend: _____

nonfiction: _____

fiction: _____

Cumulative Review

4. Refer to the selection "Cooking With Care" (page 41). According to the author, what are the four main reasons people like to cook?

1) _____

2) _____

3) _____

4) _____

5. Give three examples of foods that are high in fiber.

1) _____ 2) _____ 3) _____

6. In the selection "The French Eat Differently" (page 45), the author discusses several differences between the French diet and the American diet. Write a paragraph discussing these differences.

_____

_____

_____

_____

7. What was the main responsibility of each god or goddess?

Jupiter _____ Apollo _____

Ceres _____ Venus _____

8. What is the moral of the story of Apollo and Phaethon?

_____

_____

9. According to the story of Proserpine, Pluto and Ceres, what occurs on a regular basis due to the agreement between Pluto and Jupiter?

_____

Name: _____

Cumulative Review

10. List at least one major accomplishment of each of the following artists.

   Leonardo da Vinci _____

   Michelangelo _____

   Rembrandt _____

11. What does it mean to "counterfeit" a stamp?

   _____

12. List at least one fact about each of the following ships.

   Titanic _____

   Lusitania _____

   Virginia _____

   Monitor _____

   Constitution _____

13. Write three reasons why many big cats are endangered today.

   1) _____

   2) _____

   3) _____

14. Why is it important to "study the market" before trying to have a piece of writing published?

   _____

15. What are the names of three magazines that publish children's writing?

   1) _____

   2) _____

   3) _____

Glossary

Comprehension: Understanding what is seen, heard or read.

Context: The rest of the words in a sentence or the sentences before or after a word that help show its meaning.

Context Clues: Words that help you figure out the meaning of a word by relating it to other words in the sentence.

Fact: Information that can be proven true.

Following Directions: Doing what the directions say to do, step by step, in the correct order.

Guide Words: The words that appear at the top of dictionary pages, which tell the first and last words on each page.

Main Idea: The most important idea, or main point, in a sentence, paragraph or story.

Opinion: Information that tells how someone feels or what he/she thinks about something or someone.

Prior Knowledge: What one already knows to find an answer or get information.

Recalling Details: Being able to pick out and remember the who, what, when, where, why and how of what is read.

Sequencing: Placing events or objects in the correct order.

Summary: A short description of what a selection or book is about.

Venn Diagram: A diagram used to chart information that shows similarities and differences between two things.

Answer Key

Comprehension and Context

Comprehension is understanding what is seen, heard or read.

Context is the rest of the words in a sentence or the sentences before or after a word. Context can help with comprehension.

Context clues help you figure out the meaning of a word by relating it to other words in the sentence.

Directions: Use the context clues in the sentences to find the meanings of the bold words.

1. Jane was a **wizard** at games. She mastered them in no time and seldom lost.
   - ☐ evil magician
   - ☒ gifted person
   - ☐ average player

2. The holiday was so special that she was sure she'd never forget it. The memory would be **imprinted** forever on her mind.
   - ☐ found
   - ☐ weighed
   - ☒ fixed

3. "John will believe anything anyone tells him," his teacher said. "He's a very **impressionable** young man."
   - ☒ easily influenced
   - ☐ unhappy
   - ☐ unintelligent

4. "Do you really think it's **prudent** to spend all your money on clothes?" his mother asked crossly.
   - ☐ foolish
   - ☒ wise
   - ☐ funny

5. "Your plan has **merit**," Elizabeth's father said. "Let me give it some thought."
   - ☒ value
   - ☐ awards
   - ☐ kindness

6. John was very **gregarious** and loved being around people.
   - ☐ shy
   - ☒ outgoing
   - ☐ unfriendly

3

Comprehension: Word Origins

Did you ever wonder why we call our mid-day meal "lunch"? Or where the name "Abraham" came from? Or why one of our lovely eastern states is called "Vermont"?

These and other words have a history. The study of where words came from and how they began is called **etymology** (ett-a-mol-o-gee).

The word **lunch** comes from the Spanish word **lonjia**, which means "a slice of ham." Long ago, Spanish people ate a slice of ham for their mid-day meal. Eventually, what they ate became the word for the meal itself. Still later, it came to be pronounced "lunch" in English.

Abraham also has an interesting history. Originally, it came from the Hebrew word **avaraherm**. Abraham means "father of many."

City and state names are often based on the names of Native American tribes or describe the geography of the area. **Vermont** is actually made from two French words. **Vert** is French for "green." **Mont** is French for "mountain."

Directions: Answer these questions about word origins.

1. What is the study of the history and origin of words? _etymology_
2. From which language did the word **lunch** come? _Spanish_
3. What is the French word for "green"? _vert_
4. **Vermont** comes from two words of what language?
   - ☐ Spanish
   - ☐ English
   - ☒ French
5. Which is not correct about the origin of names of cities and states?
   - ☐ They describe geography.
   - ☐ They name Native American tribes.
   - ☒ They are mostly French in origin.

4

Fact or Opinion?

A **fact** is information that can be proven true. An **opinion** is information that tells how someone feels or what he/she thinks about something or someone.

Directions: Read the paragraph below. Then, in the corresponding numbered blanks, write whether each numbered sentence is a fact or an opinion.

(1) What to do about homeless people has become an important issue in most big cities. **(2)** Some people believe federal money should be spent to provide housing. **(3)** Others think these people should somehow find a way to take care of themselves. **(4)** Among those raising money for the homeless are bookstores. **(5)** In Los Angeles, for example, a group called "Booksellers and Writers Against Homelessness" held a series of fund-raisers for homeless people. **(6)** What a wonderful thing for these people to do! **(7)** The *Los Angeles Daily News* has helped bring public attention to the homeless through a front-page article. **(8)** The article told about a shelter for homeless women in the San Fernando Valley that was in desperate need of funds. **(9)** As a result of the article, hundreds of people sent donations to the shelter. **(10)** Americans are very generous!

1. _fact_
2. _opinion_
3. _opinion_
4. _fact_
5. _fact_
6. _opinion_
7. _fact_
8. _fact_
9. _fact_
10. _opinion_

5

Main Idea

The **main idea** is the most important idea, or main point, in a sentence, paragraph or story.

Directions: Read the paragraphs below. For each paragraph, underline the sentence that tells the main idea.

Sometimes people think they have to choose between exercise and fun. For many people, it is more fun to watch television than to run 5 miles. Yet, if you don't exercise, your body gets soft and out of shape. You move more slowly. You may even think more slowly. But why do something that isn't fun? Well, there are many ways to exercise and have fun.

One family solved the exercise problem by using their TV. They hooked up the television to an electric generator. The generator was operated by an exercise bike. Anyone who wanted to watch TV had to ride the bike. The room with their television in it must have been quite a sight!

Think of the times when you are just "hanging out" with your friends. You go outside and jump rope, play ball, run races, and so on. Soon you are all laughing and having a good time. Many group activities can provide you with exercise and be fun, too.

Maybe there aren't enough kids around after school for group games. Perhaps you are by yourself. Then what? You can get plenty of exercise just by walking, biking or even dancing. In the morning, walk the long way to the bus. Ride your bike to and from school. Practice the newest dance by yourself. Before you know it, you will be the fittest dancer of all your friends!

Directions: Write other ideas you have for combining fun and exercise below.

Answers will vary.

6

Using the Dictionary

Guide words are the words that appear at the top of dictionary pages. They show the first and last words on each page.

Directions: Read the guide words on each dictionary page below. Then look around for objects whose names come between the guide words. Write the names of the objects, and then number them in alphabetical order.

babble	buzz	magic	myself
cabin	cycle	pea	puzzle
dairy	dwarf	scar	sword
feast	future	tack	truth

Answers will vary.

7

Writing a Summary

Directions: Read the following selection. Using page 8 as a guide, write a summary of the selection.

Man's First Flights

In the first few years of the 20th century, the majority of people strongly believed that man could not and would not ever be able to fly. There were a few daring individuals who worked to prove the public wrong.

On December 8, 1903, Samuel Langley attempted to fly his version of an airplane from the roof of a houseboat on the Potomac River. Langley happened to be the secretary of the Smithsonian Institution, so his flight was covered not only by news reporters but also by government officials. Unfortunately, his trip met with sudden disaster when his aircraft did a nose dive into the river.

Nine days later, brothers Orville and Wilbur Wright attempted a flight. They had assembled their aircraft at their home in Dayton, Ohio, and shipped it to Kitty Hawk, North Carolina. On December 17, the Wright brothers made several flights, the longest one lasting an incredible 59 seconds. Since the Wright brothers had kept their flight attempts secret, their miraculous flight was only reported by two newspapers in the United States.

Answers will vary.

9

Comprehension Crossword

Directions: Use the clues from the box to complete the crossword puzzle.

```
S U M M A R Y
E         A
Q   D     I
U   I     N
E   R     I
N   E     D
COMPREHENSION
C   C     E
E   T     A
  CONTEXT
  I         FACT
OPINION
```

sequence
summary
context
comprehension
opinion
main idea
direction
fact

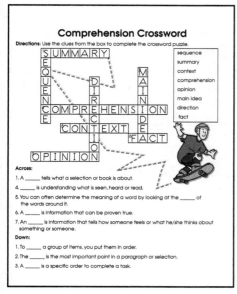

Across:
1. A _____ tells what a selection or book is about.
4. _____ is understanding what is seen, heard or read.
5. You can often determine the meaning of a word by looking at the _____ of the words around it.
6. A _____ is information that can be proven true.
7. An _____ is information that tells how someone feels or what he/she thinks about something or someone.

Down:
1. To _____ a group of items, you put them in order.
2. The _____ is the most important point in a paragraph or selection.
3. A _____ is a specific order to complete a task.

10

Using Prior Knowledge: Music

Using **prior knowledge** means being able to use what one already knows to find an answer or get information.

Directions: Before reading about music in the following section, answer these questions.

1. In your opinion, why is music important to people?

_____

2. Name as many styles of music as you can.

_____

3. What is your favorite

> Answers will vary.

4. If you could choose a musical instrument to play, what would it be? Why?

_____

5. Name a famous musician and describe what you know about him/her.

_____

11

Main Idea: Where Did Songs Come From?

Historians say the earliest music was probably connected to religion. Long ago, people believed the world was controlled by a variety of gods. Singing was among the first things humans did to show respect to the gods.

Singing is still an important part of most religions. Buddhists (bood-ists), Christians and Jews all use chants and/or songs in their religious ceremonies. If you have ever sung a song—religious or otherwise—you know that singing is fun. The feeling of joy that comes from singing must also have made ancient people feel happy.

Another time people sang was when they worked. Egyptian slaves sang as they carried the heavy stones to build the pyramids. Soldiers sang as they marched into battle. Farmers sang one song as they planted and another when they harvested. Singing made the work less burdensome. People used the tunes to pace themselves. Sometimes they followed instructions through songs. For example, "Yo-oh, heave ho!/Yo-oh, heave ho!" was sung when sailors pulled on a ship's ropes to lift the sails. **Heave** means "to lift," and that is what they did as they sang the song. The song helped sailors work together and pull at the same time. This made the task easier.

Directions: Answer these questions about music.

1. Circle the main idea:

Singing is fun, and that is why early people liked it so much.

Singing is a way to show respect to the gods and is still an important part of most religious ceremonies.

(Traditionally, singing has been important as a part of religious ceremonies and as inspiration for workers.)

> Sample answers:

2. Besides religious ceremonies, what other activity fostered singing?
   working, marching into battle, planting, harvesting

3. When did farmers sing two different songs? planting and harvesting

4. How did singing "Yo-oh, heave ho!" help sailors work? The song helped them work together to pull the ropes at the same time.

12

Comprehension: Facts About Folk Music

Folk music literally means music "of the folks," and it belongs to everyone. The names of the musicians who composed most folk music have long been forgotten. Even so, folk music has remained popular because it tells about the lives of people. Usually, the tune is simple, and even though folk songs often have many verses, the words are easy to remember. Do you know the words to "She'll Be Comin' 'Round the Mountain"?

Although no one ever says who "she" is, the verses tell you that she will be "riding six white horses" and that "we'll go out to greet her." The song also describes what will be eaten when she comes (chicken and dumplings) and what those singing will be wearing (red pajamas).

"Clementine" is a song that came out of the California gold rush in the mid-1800s. It tells the story of a woman who was "lost and gone forever" when she was killed. ("In a cavern, in a canyon, excavating for a mine/Met a miner '49er and his daughter, Clementine.")

Another famous folk song is "Swing Low, Sweet Chariot." This song was sung by slaves in the United States and today is sung by people of all races. The words "Swing low, sweet chariot, coming for to carry me home . . ." describe the soul being united with God after death. Like other folk songs that sprang from slaves, "Swing Low, Sweet Chariot" is simple, moving and powerful.

Directions: Answer these questions about folk music.

1. What is the purpose of folk music? It tells about people's lives.

_____

2. What food is sung about in "She'll Be Comin' 'Round the Mountain"? chicken and dumplings

3. Where did Clementine live?
   ☐ Florida   ☐ Mississippi   ☒ California

4. Where in the United States do you think "Swing Low, Sweet Chariot" was first sung?
   ☐ the North   ☐ the West   ☒ the South

13

Recalling Details: "Little Tommy Tucker"

Recalling details means to be able to pick out and remember the who, what, when, where, why and how of what is being read.

Little Tommy Tucker
Sings for his supper.
What shall he eat?
Brown bread and butter.
How shall he cut it
Without any knife?
How shall he marry
Without any wife?

Directions: Answer these questions about "Little Tommy Tucker."

1. What does Tommy have to do to get his supper? sing

_____

2. What does he eat for supper? brown bread and butter

_____

3. What two things does Tommy not have? a knife, a wife

14

Comprehension: Jazz Notes

Jazz, which began in the southern United States, became popular in the late 1800s. Like some folk songs, jazz was the music made by African American people. It was the music of former slaves.

The rhythm and the beat of early jazz reflected the roots of black Americans in Africa. Many early jazz musicians could not read music. They sometimes made up their music as they went along on their clarinets, trumpets and other instruments. This "on-the-spot composing" is called "improvising." Modern jazz musicians carry on this tradition of improvising. To improvise, a musician's grasp of music must go far beyond technical understanding. People used to watch jazz musicians at work, you know the effort and joy they put into their music is enormous. Two of the most famous jazz musicians are the trumpet players Louis Armstrong and Miles Davis.

Jazz is often upbeat. It reflects the musicians' joy in living. Have you ever heard the expression "Let's jazz this up"? To "jazz up" means to make something livelier. Even if you have never heard jazz played, you can imagine that it is anything but dreary!

Four to 10 musicians usually make up a jazz band. Besides the trumpet and clarinet, a jazz band may also include drums, piano, bass guitar, and sometimes a saxophone, violin and flute.

Directions: Answer these questions about jazz music.

1. What does **improvise** mean? on-the-spot composing

2. Why did early jazz musicians improvise? They could not read music.

_____

3. Name two famous jazz musicians. Louis Armstrong and Miles Davis

4. Jazz music is   ☐ slow.   ☒ upbeat.   ☐ dreary.

5. Which of the following is not a jazz instrument?
   ☐ drum   ☐ piano   ☒ organ   ☐ violin   ☐ flute

15

Recalling Details: Woodwinds

There are four kinds of woodwind instruments in modern bands. They are flutes, oboes, clarinets and bassoons. They are called "woodwind" instruments for two sensible reasons. In the beginning, they were all made of wood. Also, the musician's breath, or "wind," was required to play them.

Although they are all woodwinds, these instruments look different and are played differently. To play an oboe, the musician blows through a mouthpiece on the front of the instrument. The mouthpiece, called a reed, is made of two flat pieces of a kind of wood called cane. Clarinet players also blow into a reed mouthpiece. The clarinet has only one reed in its mouthpiece.

To play the flute, the musician blows across a hole near one end of the instrument. The way the breath is aimed helps to make the flute's different sounds. The bassoon is the largest woodwind instrument. Bassoon players blow through a mouthpiece that goes through a short metal pipe before it goes into the body of the bassoon. It makes a very different sound from the clarinet or the oboe.

Woodwind instruments also have keys—but not the kind of keys that open locks. These keys are more like levers that the musician pushes up and down. The levers cover holes. When the musician pushes down on a lever, it closes that hole. When he/she lifts his/her finger, it opens the hole. Different sounds are produced by controlling the amount of breath, or "wind," that goes through the holes.

Directions: Answer these questions about woodwind instruments.

1. What instruments are in the woodwind section? oboe, clarinet, flute, bassoon

2. Why are some instruments called woodwinds? In the beginning, they were all made of wood. They require "breath" to play them.

3. How is a flute different from the other woodwinds? It does not have a mouthpiece.

4. What happens when a musician pushes down on a woodwind key? It covers a hole in the instrument.

5. How would a woodwind musician open the holes on his/her instrument? lift his/her finger

16

Comprehension: Harp Happenings

If you have ever heard a harpist play, you know what a lovely sound a harp makes. Music experts say the harp is among the oldest of instruments. It probably was invented several thousand years ago in or near Egypt.

The first harps are believed to have been made by stretching a string tightly between an empty tortoise shell and a curved pole. The empty shell magnified the sound the string made when it was plucked. More strings were added later so that more sounds could be made. Over the centuries, the shape of the harp gradually was changed into that of the large, graceful instruments we recognize today.

Here is how a harpist plays a harp. First, he/she leans the harp against his/her right shoulder. Then, the harpist puts his/her hands on either side of the harp and plucks its strings with both hands.

A harp has seven pedals on the bottom back. The audience usually cannot see these pedals. Most people are surprised to learn about them. The pedals are connected to the strings. Stepping on a particular pedal causes certain strings to tighten. The tightening and loosening of the strings makes different sounds; so does the way the strings are plucked with the hands.

At first glance, harps look like simple instruments. Actually, they are rather complicated and difficult to keep in tune. A harpist often spends as long as half an hour before a performance tuning his/her harp's strings so it produces the correct sounds.

Directions: Answer these questions about harps.

1. When were harps invented? several thousand years ago

2. Where were harps invented? in or near Egypt

3. What is a person called who plays the harp? harpist

4. The harpist leans the harp against his/her
   ☒ right shoulder. ☐ left shoulder. ☐ left knee.

5. How many pedals does a harp have?
   ☐ five ☐ six ☒ seven

6. Harps are easy to play.
   ☐ yes ☒ no

17

Comprehension: Brass Shows Class

If you like band music, you probably love the music made by brass instruments. Bright, loud, moving and magnificent—all these words describe the sounds made by brass.

Some of the earliest instruments were horns. Made from hollowed-out animal horns, these primitive instruments could not possibly have made the rich sounds of modern horns that are made of brass.

Most modern brass bands have three instruments—tubas, trombones and trumpets. Combined, these instruments can produce stirring marches, as well as haunting melodies. The most famous composer for brass instruments was John Phillip Sousa. Born in Washington, D.C., in 1854, Sousa was a military band conductor and composer. He died in 1932, but his music is still very popular today. One of Sousa's most famous tunes for military bands is "Stars and Stripes Forever."

Besides composing band music, Sousa also invented a practical band instrument—the sousaphone. The sousaphone is a huge tuba that makes very low noises. Because of the way it curls around the body, a sousaphone is easier to carry than a tuba, especially when the musician must march. This is exactly why John Phillip Sousa invented it!

Directions: Answer these questions about brass instruments.

1. Who invented the sousaphone? John Phillip Sousa

2. What were the first horns made from? hollowed-out animal horns

3. Where was John Phillip Sousa born? Washington, D.C.

4. When did John Phillip Sousa die? 1932

5. Why did Sousa invent the sousaphone? It was easier to carry than a tuba.

6. What types of instruments make up a modern brass band? tubas, trombones and trumpets

18

Comprehension: Violins

If you know anything about violin music, chances are you have heard the word **Stradivarius** (Strad-uh-vary-us). Stradivarius is the name for the world's most magnificent violins. They are named after their creator, Antonio Stradivari.

Stradivari was born in northern Italy and lived from 1644 to 1737. Cremona, the town he lived in, was a place where violins were manufactured. Stradivari was very young when he learned to play the violin. He grew to love the instrument so much that he began to make them himself.

Violins were new instruments during Stradivari's time. People made them in different sizes and shapes and of different types of wood. Stradivari is said to have been very particular about the wood he selected for his violins. He took long walks alone in the forest to find just the right tree. He is also said to have used a secret and special type of varnish to put on the wood. Whatever the reasons, his violins are the best in the world.

Stradivari put such care and love into his violins that they are still used today. Many of these are in museums. But some wealthy musicians, who can afford the thousands and thousands of dollars they cost, own Stradivarius violins.

Stradivari passed his methods on to his sons. But the secrets of making Stradivarius violins seem to have died out with the family. Their rarity, as well as their mellow sound, make Stradivarius violins among the most prized instruments in the world.

Directions: Answer these questions about Stradivarius violins.

1. Where did Stradivari live? Cremona

2. Why did he begin making violins? because he loved them so much

3. Why are Stradivarius violins special? He used special wood and varnish.

4. Where can Stradivarius violins be found today? museums and some wealthy musicians

5. How did Stradivari select the wood for his violins? He took long walks alone in the forest to find just the right tree.

6. Who else knew Stradivari's secrets for making such superior violins? his sons

19

Review

Directions: Complete the following exercises.

1. Write a four-sentence summary of the selection "Where Did Songs Come From?" (page 12).

   Answers will vary.

2. Describe the main difference between a clarinet and an oboe.

   The oboe has two reeds in its mouthpiece while the clarinet has only one.

3. How do the keys of woodwind instruments work?

   The keys are like levers that, when pressed, cover a hole in the instrument. This changes the sound.

4. Write a summary of the history of the harp.

   Answers will vary.

5. Define the following words from the selection "Facts About Folk Music" (page 13).

   verses: stanza of a poem or a song

   excavating: make a hole or channel by digging

   chariot: two-wheeled vehicle drawn by a horse

   composed: created in music or writing

20

Using Prior Knowledge: Farm Animals

Directions: Before reading about farm animals in the following section, answer these questions.

1. List at least nine types of farm animals by mother and baby names.

   Example: sow—piglet

   _____ _____

   _____ _____

   _____ _____

   _____ _____

2. If you owned a large ranch, what type of livestock would you enjoy keeping? Why?

   Answers will vary.

3. Some animals give birth to more than one.

4. Would you enjoy living on a farm? Why or why not?

   _____

   _____

5. What is the importance of raising livestock today?

   _____

   _____

21

Sequencing: "Little Bo-Peep"

Sequencing means placing events or objects in the correct order.

Directions: Read "Little Bo-Peep." Then number the events in the poem in the correct order.

Little Bo-Peep has lost her sheep,
And can't tell where to find them.
"I'll leave them alone, and they'll come home,
Wagging their tails behind them."

Then Little Bo-Peep dreamed of her sheep,
She dreamed she heard the bleating.
But when she awoke, she found it a joke,
For they were still a-fleeting.

Then up she took her little crook,
Determined for to find them.
She found them indeed,
But it made her heart bleed,
For they'd left their tails behind them!

It happened one day that Bo-Peep did stray
Into a meadow nearby,
She looked up in a tree, and what did she see?
Their tails all hung out to dry!

Bo-Peep heaved a sigh and looked to the sky
As she gathered their tails up fast.
She ran to her sheep, they all gave a bleat
And said, "Our tails are back at last!"

6 Little Bo-Peep returned her sheep's tails to them.
2 Little Bo-Peep decided her sheep would find their way home.
1 Little Bo-Peep lost her sheep.
3 Little Bo-Peep dreamed about her sheep.
4 Little Bo-Peep found her sheep.
5 Little Bo-Peep found her sheeps' tails in a tree.

22

Comprehension: All About Sheep

Did you ever wonder what really happened to the tails of Little Bo-Peep's sheep? Here's the real story.

When sheep are born, they are called lambs. Lambs are born with long tails. A few days after lambs are born, the shepherd cuts off their tails. Because they get dirty, the lambs' long tails can pick up lots of germs. Cutting them off helps to prevent disease. The procedure is called "docking." This is probably what happened to Bo-Peep's sheep! Another shepherd must have cut their tails off without telling her.

Little lambs are cute. A lamb grows inside its mother for 150 days before it is born. This is called the "gestation period." Some types of sheep, such as hill sheep, give birth to one lamb at a time. Other types of sheep, such as lowland sheep, give birth to two or three lambs at a time.

After it is born, it takes a lamb 3 or 4 days to recognize its mother. Once it does, it stays close to her until it is about 3 weeks old. After that, the lamb becomes friendly toward other lambs.

Young lambs then form play groups. They chase each other in circles. They butt into each other. Like children, they pretend to fight. When play gets too rough, the lambs run back to their mothers for protection.

Lambs follow their mothers as they graze on grass. Usually, sheep move in single file behind an older female sheep. Female sheep are called ewes. The ewes teach their lambs how to keep themselves clean. This is called "grooming." Sheep groom only their faces. Here is how they do it: They lick one of their front legs, then they rub their faces against the spot they have licked.

Directions: Follow the instructions below.

1. Define the word **docking**. to cut off the lamb's tail
2. Name a type of sheep that gives birth to one lamb at a time. hill sheep
3. Name a type of sheep that gives birth to two or three lambs at a time.
   lowland sheep
4. Female sheep are called
   ☐ grazers. ☒ ewes. ☐ dockers.
5. Lambs begin playing in groups when they are
   ☐ 2 weeks old. ☒ 3 weeks old. ☐ 4 weeks old.

23

Recalling Details: "Little Boy Blue"

Directions: Read "Little Boy Blue." Then complete the puzzle.

Little Boy Blue, come blow your horn.
The sheep's in the meadow, the cow's in the corn;
But where is the boy who looks after the sheep?
He's under a haystack, fast asleep!
Will you awake him? No, not I.
For if I do, he's sure to cry.

Crossword:
Across: MEADOW, HORN, ASLEEP, AWAKE
Down: HAYSTACK, CORN, SHEEP, NO

Across:
3. This is where the sheep was.
5. What Little Boy Blue was asked to blow.
7. The other boy was fast _____.
8. Little Boy Blue was not asleep. He was _____.

Down:
1. The boy who looks after the sheep slept here.
2. This is what the cow got into.
4. This is what the boy was supposed to be tending.
6. Did they wake the sleeping boy?

24

Comprehension: Pigs Are Particular

Have you ever wondered why pigs wallow in the mud? It's not because they are dirty animals. Pigs have no sweat glands. They can't sweat, so they roll in the mud to cool themselves. The next time you hear anyone who's hot say, "I'm sweating like a pig!" be sure to correct him/her. Humans can sweat but pigs cannot.

Actually, pigs are particular about their pens. They are very clean animals. They prefer to sleep in clean, dry places. They move their bowels and empty their bladders in another area. They do not want to get their homes dirty.

Another misconception about pigs is that they are smooth. Only cartoon pigs are pink, smooth and shiny-looking. The skin of real pigs is covered with bristles—small, stiff hairs. Their bristles protect their tender skin. When pigs are slaughtered, their bristles are sometimes made into hair brushes or clothes brushes.

Female pigs are called sows. Sows have babies twice a year and give birth to 10 to 14 piglets at a time. The babies have a "gestation period" of 16 weeks before they are born.

All the piglets together are called a "litter." Newborn piglets are on their tiny feet within a few minutes after birth. Can you guess why? They are hungrily looking for their mother's teats so they can get milk. As they nurse, piglets snuggle in close to their mother's belly to keep warm.

Directions: Answer these questions about pigs.

1. Why do pigs wallow in mud? to cool off
2. How long is the gestation period for pigs? 16 weeks
3. What are pig bristles used for? to protect their skin
4. Tell two reasons pigs are on their feet soon after they are born.
   1) to get milk   2) to get warm
5. A female pig is called a
   ☐ bristle. ☐ piglet. ☒ sow.
6. Together, the newborn piglets are called a
   ☐ group. ☐ family. ☒ litter.

25

Context Clues: No Kidding About Goats

Goats are independent creatures. Unlike sheep, which move easily in herds, goats cannot be driven along by a goatherd. They must be moved one or two at a time. Moving a big herd of goats can take a long time, and goatherds must be patient people.

Both male and female goats can have horns, but some goats don't have them at all. Male goats have beards but females do not. Male goats also have thicker and shaggier coats than females. During breeding season, male goats have a very strong smell.

Goats are kept in paddocks with high fences. The fences are high because goats are good jumpers. They like to nibble on hedges and on the tips of young trees. They can cause a lot of damage this way! That is why many farmers keep their goats in a paddock.

Baby goats are called "kids," and two or three at a time are born to the mother goat. Farmers usually begin to bottle-feed kids when they are a few days old. They milk the mother goat and keep the milk. Goat's milk is much easier to digest than cow's milk, and many people think it tastes delicious.

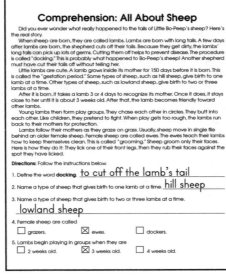

Directions: Answer these questions about goats.

1. Use context clues to choose the correct definition of **goatherd**.
   ☒ person who herds goats ☐ goats in a herd ☐ person who has heard of goats
2. Use context clues to choose the correct definition of **paddock**.
   ☐ pad ☐ fence ☒ pen
3. Use context clues to choose the correct definition of **nibble**.
   ☒ take small bites ☐ take small drinks ☐ take little sniffs
4. Use context clues to choose the correct definition of **delicious**.
   ☐ delicate ☒ tasty ☐ terrible

26

Comprehension: Cows Are Complicated

If you believe cows have four stomachs, you're right! It sounds incredible, but it's true.

Here are the "hows" and "whys" of a cow's digestive system. First, it's important to know that cows do not have front teeth. They eat grass by wrapping their tongues around it and pulling it from the ground. They do have back teeth, but still they cannot properly chew the grass.

Cows swallow grass without chewing. When it's swallowed, the grass goes into the cow's first stomach, called a "rumen" (roo-mun). There it is broken up by the digestive juices and forms into a ball of grass. This ball is called a "cud." The cow is able to bring the cud back up into its mouth. Then the cow chews the cud into a pulp with its back teeth and re-swallows it.

After it is swallowed the second time, the cud goes into the cow's second stomach. This second stomach is called the "reticulum" (re-tick-u-lum). The reticulum filters the food to sort out any small stones or other non-food matter. Then it passes the food onto the cow's third stomach. The third stomach is called the "omasum" (oh-mass-um).

From there, any food that is still undigested is sent back to the first stomach so the cow can bring it back up into her mouth and chew it some more. The rest goes into the cow's fourth stomach. The fourth stomach is called the "abomasum" (ab-oh-ma-sum). Digesting food that can be turned into milk is a full-time job for cows!

Directions: Answer these questions about cows.

1. List in order the names of a cow's four stomachs.
   1) rumen 2) reticulum 3) omasum 4) abomasum
2. What is the name of the ball of grass a cow chews on? cud
3. A cow has no
   ☒ front teeth. ☐ back teeth. ☐ fourth stomach.
4. Which stomach acts as a filter for digestion?
   ☒ reticulum ☐ rumen ☐ abomasum

27

Context Clues: Dairy Cows

Some cows are raised for their beef. Other cows, called dairy cows, are raised for their milk. A dairy cow cannot produce any milk until after its first calf is born. Cows are not mature enough to give birth until they are 2 years old. A cow's gestation period is 40 weeks long, and she usually gives birth to one calf. Then she produces a lot of milk to feed it. When the calf is 2 days old, the dairy farmer takes the calf away from its mother. After that, the cow is milked twice a day.

The dairy cow's milk comes from the large, smooth udder beneath her body. The udder has four openings called "teats." To milk the cow, the farmer grasps a teat and squeezes it with his thumb and forefinger. Then he gently but firmly pulls his hand down the teat to squeeze the milk out. Milking machines that are hooked to the cow's teats duplicate this action and can milk many cows quickly.

A dairy cow's milk production is not at the same level all the time. When the cow is pregnant, milk production gradually decreases. For 2 months before her calf is born, a cow is said to be "dry" and is not milked. This happens because, like humans, much of the cow's food is actually being used to nourish the unborn calf.

Farmers give the cow extra food at this time to make sure the mother and unborn calf are well-nourished. Again, like humans, well-nourished mother cows are more likely to produce healthy babies.

Directions: Answer these questions about dairy cows.

1. Use context clues to choose the correct definition of **grasp**.
☐ pull firmly ☒ hold firmly ☐ hold gently

2. Use context clues to choose the correct definition of **duplicate**.
☐ correct ☐ make ☒ copy

3. Use context clues to choose the correct definition of **decrease**.
☐ become more ☒ become less ☐ become quicker

4. Use context clues to choose the correct definition of **nourish**.
☐ to be happy ☐ to be friendly ☒ to feed

28

Comprehension: Chickens

Have you ever heard the expression "pecking order"? In the pecking order of a school, the principal is at the top of the order. Next comes the assistant principal, then the teachers and students.

In the pecking order of chickens, the most aggressive chicken is the leader. The leader is the hen that uses her beak most often to peck the chickens she bosses. These chickens, in turn, boss other chickens by pecking them, and so on. Chickens can peck all others who are "below" them in the pecking order. They never peck "above" themselves by pecking their bosses.

Answer these questions about chickens.

1. Put this pecking order of four chickens in order.
2 This chicken pecks numbers 3 and 4 but never 1.
1 No one pecks this chicken. She's the top boss.
4 This chicken can't peck anyone.
3 This chicken pecks chicken number 4.

2. Use context clues to figure out the definition of **aggressive**.
Answers will vary.

3. Who is at the top of the pecking order in a scho Answers may include:
principal

29

Review

Directions: Follow the instructions for each section.

1. Write a summary of the selection "All About Sheep" (page 23).
Answers will vary.

2. What is the purpose of a pig's bristles?
The bristles protect their skin.

3. Write a summary of the selection "No Kidding About Goats" (page 26).
Answers will vary.

4. What is the purpose of a cow's four stomachs?
digest food that can be turned into milk

5. How do chickens establish leaders and followers?
Chickens peck each other to determine dominance. Chickens will only peck another chicken who is "below" them.

6. What is a "cud"?
the ball of grass formed by the rumen

30

Review

Directions: Define the following words from this section.

1. bleating:
2. graze:
3. wallow:
4. gestation:
5. independent:
6. paddock:
7. digest:
8. rumen:
9. reticulum: Answers will vary.
10. omasum:
11. abomasum:
12. pulp:
13. duplicate:
14. nourish:
15. aggressive:

Directions: Choose four words from above and use each in a sentence.

1.
2.
3.
4.

31

Using Prior Knowledge: Books

Directions: Before reading about books in the following section, answer these questions.

1. What books have you read recently?

2. Write a summary of one of the b
Answers will vary.

3. Define the following types of books and, if possible, give an example of each.
biography: story of a person's life, told by another Examples will vary.
fiction: non-factual literature
mystery: dealing with a puzzling event
nonfiction: a literary work other than fiction

32

Context Clues: Remember Who You Are

Directions: Read each paragraph. Then use context clues to figure out the meanings of the bold words.

During the 1940s, Esther Hautzig lived in the town of Vilna, which was then part of Poland. Shortly after the **outbreak** of World War II, she and her family were **deported** to Siberia by Russian communists who hated Jews. She told what happened to her and other Polish Jews in a book. The book is called *Remember Who You Are: Stories About Being Jewish.*

1. Choose the correct definition of **deported**.
☒ sent away ☐ asked to go ☐ invited to visit

2. Choose the correct definition of **outbreak**.
☒ a sudden occurrence ☐ to leave suddenly

Remember Who You Are: Stories About Being Jewish is a nonfiction book that tells true stories. An interesting **fiction** book is *Leave the Cooking to Me* by Judie Angell. It tells the story of a girl named Shirley, who learns about cooking from her best friend's mother. Most young people have a hard time finding jobs that pay well, but Shirley's cooking skills help her land a **lucrative** summer job.

3. Choose the correct definition of **fiction**.
☐ stories that are true ☒ stories that are not true

4. Choose the correct definition of **lucrative**.
☐ interesting ☒ profitable ☐ nearby

33

Comprehension: Books and More Books!

Variety is said to be the spice of life. Where books are concerned, variety is the key to reading pleasure. There is a type of book that appeals to every reader.

Each year, hundreds of new books are published for children. A popular series of books for girls between the ages of 8 and 12 is *Sweet Valley Kids*, written by Francine Pascal. All of Pascal's books are fictional stories about children who live in the town of Sweet Valley.

If you like legends, an interesting book is *Dream Wolf* by Paul Goble. *Dream Wolf* is a retelling of an old Native American legend. Legends are stories passed down from one generation to another that may or may not be true. Some of them are scary! *The Legend of Sleepy Hollow*, for example, is about a headless horseman. Other legends are about a person's brave or amazing deeds. For example, there are many legends about Robin Hood, who stole from the rich and gave to the poor.

Many people like to read nonfiction books, which are about things that really exist or really happened. Many children who like nonfiction choose books about animals, careers, sports and hobbies. Those interested in information about Native Americans might like to read these books: *The Navajos* by Peter Iverson, *The Yakima* by Helen Schuster and *The Creek* by Michael Green. The titles of these nonfiction books are names of Native American tribes.

Directions: Answer these questions about different types of books.

1. What is the name of Francine Pascal's book series? *Sweet Valley Kids*

2. What legend is about a headless horseman? *Legend of Sleepy Hollow*

3. Which of the following is not correct about legends?

☐ Legends are passed down through the generations.

☒ All legends are scary.

☐ Some legends are about people who did braves things.

34

Comprehension: Help for the Homeless

In Dayton, Ohio, a bookstore called Books & Co. launched a program to educate the public about the needs of homeless people. The program was built around profits from sales of a book called *Louder Than Words*. The book is a collection of 22 short stories by such noted authors as Louise Erdrich and Anne Tyler.

Many of the authors helped promote the book by coming to the bookstore to autograph copies of *Louder Than Words*. All profits from the sale of the book were donated to a fund that provides food and housing for homeless people.

The fund for the homeless is managed by a nonprofit organization called Share Our Strength. Located in Washington, D.C., the organization distributes the money to food banks and shelters for homeless people around the United States.

By the end of 1990, $50,000 had been raised for the homeless from the sale of *Louder Than Words*. Other bookstore owners learned about the success of Books & Co. in raising money for the homeless. They were impressed! Now, bookstores in these other cities are running fund-raising efforts of their own: Ann Arbor, Michigan; Columbus, Ohio; Taos, New Mexico; and Minneapolis, Minnesota.

Directions: Answer these questions about how booksellers have helped raise funds for the homeless.

1. How many short stories are in the book *Louder Than Words*? 22

2. What is the name of the organization that distributes money to homeless shelters around the country? Share Our Strength

3. Name two authors whose stories are included in *Louder Than Words*.

Louise Erdich and Anne Tyler

4. Share Our Strength is located in what city?

☐ Portland, OR   ☐ Minneapolis, MN   ☒ Washington, D.C.

5. In what city is Books & Co. located?

☐ Columbus, OH   ☒ Dayton, OH   ☐ Taos, NM

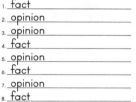

35

Fact or Opinion?

Directions: Read the paragraphs below. Then, in the corresponding numbered blanks, write whether each numbered sentence is a fact or an opinion.

Have you ever seen *Reading Rainbow* on your local public television station? **(1)** It's a show about books, and its host is LeVar Burton. **(2)** LeVar is very handsome and the show is great!

Some books that have been featured on the show are *I Can Be an Oceanographer* by Paul Sipiera, *Soccer Sam* by Jean Marzollo, *Redbird* by Patrick Fort and *Miss Nelson Has a Field Day* by Harry Allard. **(3)** *Miss Nelson Has a Field Day* sounds like the most interesting book of all!

(4) On *Reading Rainbow*, children give informal book reports about books they have read. **(5)** All the children are adorable! In about 1 minute, each child describes his or her book. **(6)** While the child is talking, pictures of some of the pages from the book are shown. **(7)** Seeing the pictures will make you want to read the book. A few books are described on each show. **(8)** Other activities include trips with LeVar to places the books tell about. **(9)** Every child should make time to watch *Reading Rainbow*! **(10)** It's a fabulous show!

1. fact
2. opinion
3. opinion
4. fact
5. opinion
6. fact
7. opinion
8. fact
9. opinion
10. opinion

36

Context Clues: Kids' Books Are Big Business

Between 1978 and 1988, the number of children's books published in the United States doubled. The publishing industry, which prints, promotes and sells books, does not usually move this fast. Why? Because if publishers print too many books that don't sell, they lose money. They like to wait, if they can, to see what the "public demand" is for certain types of books. Then they accept manuscripts from writers who have written the types of books the public seems to want. More than 4,600 children's books were published in 1988, because publishers thought they could sell that many titles. Many copies of each title were printed and sold to bookstores and libraries. The publishers made good profits and, since then, the number of children's books published each year has continued to grow.

The title of a recent new book for children is *The Wild Horses of Sweetbriar* by Natalie Kinsey-Warnock. It is the story of a girl and a band of wild horses that lived on an island off the coast of Massachusetts in 1903. The story sounds very exciting! Wild horses can be quite dangerous. The plot of *The Wild Horses of Sweetbriar* is probably filled with danger and suspense.

Directions: Answer these questions about how interest in writing, reading and selling children's books has grown.

1. Use context clues to choose the correct definition of **industry**.

☐ booksellers   ☐ writers   ☒ entire business

2. If 4,600 books were sold in 1988, how many books were sold in 1978? 2,300

3. The number of children's books published in the United States doubled between 1978 and 1988.   (Fact)   Opinion

4. *The Wild Horses of Sweetbriar* is the story of a girl and a band of wild horses that lived on an island in 1903.   (Fact)   Opinion

5. The story sounds very exciting!   Fact   (Opinion)

6. The plot of *The Wild Horses of Sweetbriar* is probably filled with danger and suspense.   Fact   (Opinion)

37

Review

Directions: Follow the instructions below.

1. Write a summary of the selection "Help for the Homeless" (page 35).

2. What skills must a writer have in order to produce a book?

3. Define the following words:

appeal:

legend:

deed:

generation:

profit:

distribute:

suspense:

manuscript:

Answers will vary.

4. Interview the members of your family. Ask each person his/her favorite book title and the reason he/she enjoyed it. Then, summarize your findings in a paragraph.

38

Using Prior Knowledge: Cooking

Before reading about cooking in the following section, answer these questions.

1. What is your favorite recipe? Why?

2. What do you most like to cook? Why?

3. Have you tried... food do you like most?

Answers will vary.

4. Why is it important to follow the correct sequence when preparing a recipe?

5. What safety precautions must be followed when working in a kitchen?

39

Following Directions: Chunky Tomato and Green Onion Sauce

Following directions means to do what the directions say to do, step by step, in the correct order.

Directions: Read the recipe for chunky tomato and green onion sauce. Answer the questions below.

Ingredients:
- 2 tablespoons corn oil
- 2 cloves of garlic, finely chopped
- 1½ pounds plum tomatoes, cored, peeled, seeded, then coarsely chopped
- 3 green onions, cut in half lengthwise, then thinly sliced
- salt
- freshly ground pepper

Heat oil in a heavy skillet over medium heat. Add garlic and cook until yellow, about 1 minute. Stir in tomatoes. Season with salt and pepper. Cook until thickened, about 10 minutes. Stir in green onions and serve.

1. What is the last thing the cook does to prepare the tomatoes before cooking them?
   chops them
2. What kind of oil does the cook heat in the heavy skillet? corn oil
3. How long should the garlic be cooked? about 1 minute
4. What does the cook do to the tomatoes right before removing the seeds?
   peels them
5. Is the sauce served hot or cold? hot

40

Comprehension: Cooking With Care

People are so busy these days that many have no time to cook. This creates a problem, because most families love home cooking! The food tastes good and warm, and a family meal brings everyone together. In some families, meals are often the only times everyone sees one another at the same time.

Another reason people enjoy home cooking is that it is often a way of showing love. A parent who bakes a batch of chocolate chip cookies isn't just satisfying a child's sweet tooth. He/she is sending a message. The message says, "I care about you enough to spend an hour making cookies that you will eat up in 15 minutes if I let you!"

There's also something about the smell of good cooking that appeals to people of all ages. It makes most of us feel secure and loved—even if we are the ones doing the cooking! Next time you smell a cake baking, stop for a moment and pay attention to your mood. Chances are, the good smell is making you feel happy.

Real estate agents know that good cooking smells are important. They sometimes advise people whose homes are for sale to bake cookies or bread if prospective buyers are coming to see the house. The good smells make the place "feel like home." These pleasant smells help convince potential buyers that the house would make a good home for their family, too!

Directions: Answer these questions about good cooking.

1. Why do fewer people cook nowadays? They are too busy
2. Why are family meals important? They bring everyone together
3. What do homemade cookies do besides satisfy a child's sweet tooth?
   Someone cared enough to spend his/her time making them.
4. Real estate agents often advise home sellers holding open houses to
   ☐ clean the garage. ☒ bake cookies or bread.
5. The smell of baking at open houses may encourage buyers to
   ☐ bake cookies. ☒ buy the house. ☐ bake bread.

41

Sequencing: Chocolate Chunk Cookies

These chocolate chunk cookies require only five ingredients. Before you combine them, preheat the oven to 350 degrees. Preheating the oven to the correct temperature is always step number one in baking.

Now, into a large mixing bowl, empty an 18¼-ounce package of chocolate fudge cake mix (any brand). Add a 10-ounce package of semi-sweet chocolate, broken into small pieces, two 5⅛-ounce packages of chocolate fudge pudding mix (any brand) and 1½ cups chopped walnuts.

Use a large wooden spoon to combine the ingredients. When they are well-mixed, add 1½ cups mayonnaise and stir thoroughly. Shape the dough into small balls and place the balls 2 inches apart on an ungreased cookie sheet. Bake 12 minutes. Cool and eat!

Directions: Number in correct order the steps for making chocolate chunk cookies.

6 Place 1½ cups of mayonnaise in the bowl.
8 Shape dough into small balls and place them on a cookie sheet.
2 Empty the package of chocolate fudge cake mix into the bowl.
9 Bake the dough for 12 minutes.
4 Place two 5⅛-ounce packages of chocolate fudge pudding in the bowl.
5 Put 1½ cups chopped walnuts in the bowl.
1 Preheat the oven to 350 degrees.
3 Place the 10-ounce package of semi-sweet chocolate pieces in the bowl.
7 Stir everything thoroughly.

42

Comprehension: Eating High-Fiber Foods

Have you heard your parents or other adults talk about "high-fiber" diets? Foods that are high in fiber, like oats and other grains, are believed to be very healthy. Here's why: The fiber adds bulk to the food the body digests and helps keep the large intestines working properly. Corn, apples, celery, nuts and other chewy foods also contain fiber that helps keep the body's systems for digesting and eliminating food working properly.

Researchers at the University of Minnesota have found another good reason to eat high-fiber food, especially at breakfast. Because fiber is bulky, it absorbs a lot of liquid in the stomach. As it absorbs the liquid, it swells. This "fools" the stomach into thinking it's full. As a result, when lunchtime comes, those who have eaten a high-fiber breakfast are not as hungry. They eat less food at lunch. Without much effort on their parts, dieters eating a high-fiber breakfast can lose weight.

The university researchers say a person could lose 10 pounds in a year just by eating a high-fiber breakfast! This is good news to people who are only slightly overweight and want an easy method for losing that extra 10 pounds.

Directions: Answer these questions about eating high-fiber foods.

1. Why is fiber healthy? It adds bulk and helps the large intestine
   work properly.
2. How does fiber "fool" the stomach? It absorbs liquid and swells.
3. How does "fooling" the stomach help people lose weight? People feel full
   and aren't as hungry.
4. How many pounds could a dieter eating a high-fiber breakfast lose in a year?
   ☐ 20 pounds ☐ 30 pounds ☒ 10 pounds
5. The university that did the research is in which state?
   ☐ Michigan ☒ Minnesota ☐ Montana

43

Main Idea: New Corn

I will clothe myself in spring clothing
And visit the slopes of the eastern hill.
By the mountain stream, a mist hovers,
Hovers a moment and then scatters.
Then comes a wind blowing from the south
That brushes the fields of new corn.

Directions: Answer these questions about this ancient poem, which is translated from Chinese.

1. Circle the main idea:
   (The poet will dress comfortably and go to where the corn grows so he/she can enjoy the beauty of nature.)

   The poet will dress comfortably and visit the slopes of the eastern hill, where he/she will plant corn.
2. From which direction does the wind blow? the south
3. Where does the mist hover? by the mountain stream
4. What do you think the poet means by "spring clothing"? Answers will vary.

44

Comprehension: The French Eat Differently

Many people believe that French people are very different from Americans. This is certainly true where eating habits are concerned! According to a report by the World Health Organization, each year the French people eat four times more butter than Americans. The French also eat twice as much cheese! In addition, they eat more vegetables, potatoes, grain and fish.

Yet, despite the fact that they eat larger amounts of these foods, the French take in about the same number of calories each day as Americans. (French and American men consume about 2,500 calories daily. French and American women take in about 1,600 calories daily.) How can this be? If the French are eating more of certain types of foods, shouldn't this add up to more calories? And why are so few French people overweight compared to Americans? The answer—Americans consume 18 times more refined sugar than the French and drink twice as much whole milk!

Although many Americans believe the French end each meal with grand and gooey desserts, this just isn't so. Except for special occasions, dessert in a typical French home consists of fresh fruit or cheese. Many American families, on the other hand, like to end their meals with a bowl or two of ice cream or another sweet treat.

It's believed that this difference in the kind of calories consumed—rather than in the total number of calories taken in—is what causes many Americans to be chubby and most French people to be thin.

Directions: Answer these questions about the eating habits of French and American people.

1. How many calories does the average French man eat each day? 2,500
2. How much whole milk does the average French person drink compared to the average American? half as much
3. How much more refined sugar do Americans eat than the French?
   ☐ 2 times more ☒ 18 times more ☐ 15 times more
4. What do French families usually eat for dessert?
   ☐ refined sugar ☐ ice cream ☒ fruit and cheese

45

Comprehension: Chinese Cabbage

Many Americans enjoy Chinese food. In big cities, like New York and Chicago, many Chinese restaurants deliver their food in small boxes to homes. It's just like ordering a pizza! Then the people who ordered the "take-out" food simply open it, put it on their plates and eat it while it's hot.

Because it tastes so good, many people are curious about the ingredients in Chinese food. Siu choy and choy sum are two types of Chinese cabbage that many people enjoy eating. Siu choy grows to be 2 to 3 feet! Of course, it is chopped into small pieces before it is cooked and served. Its leaves are light green and soft. It is not crunchy like American cabbage. Siu choy is used in soups and stews. Sometimes it is pickled with vinegar and other ingredients and served as a side dish to other courses.

Choy sum looks and tastes different from siu choy. Choy sum grows to be only 8 to 10 inches. It is a flowering cabbage that grows small yellow flowers. The flowers are "edible," which means they can be eaten. Its leaves are long and bright green. After its leaves are boiled for 4 minutes, oil is often served as a salad. Oil and oyster sauce are mixed together and poured over choy sum as a salad dressing.

Directions: Answer these questions about Chinese cabbage.

1. Which Chinese cabbage grows small yellow flowers? **choy sum**

2. Which Chinese cabbage is served as a salad? **choy sum**

3. Is siu choy crunchy? **no**

4. What ingredients are in the salad dressing used on choy sum?
oil and oyster sauce

5. To what size does siu choy grow? **2 to 3 feet**

6. Name two main dishes in which siu choy is used: **soups and stews**

46

Review

Here's a recipe for a special mashed potato treat that serves two people. The recipe is fast and easy to follow, and the results are delicious!

Begin by peeling two large potatoes and cooking them in a pot of boiling water. When a fork or knife inserted into them pulls out easily, you will know they are done. Then take them from the pot and drain them well. Place them in a large mixing bowl and add 2 tablespoons of milk and 2 tablespoons of butter. Mash with a potato masher until the lumps are gone.

In a skillet, melt a tablespoon of butter and add one bunch of chopped green onions. Cook them about 1 minute. Add them to the potatoes and mix gently. Season with salt and pepper and add more butter if desired. Serve and eat!

Directions: Answer these questions about how to make mashed potatoes with green onions.

1. Circle the main idea:

(This recipe is fast and easy, and the potatoes are delicious.)

This recipe has only four ingredients (plus salt and pepper).

2. Name the main ingredients in this recipe (not including salt and pepper).
potatoes, milk, butter, green onions

3. How many people does this recipe serve? **2**

4. Number in order the steps for making mashed potatoes with green onions.

  4 Cook the chopped green onions for 1 minute.

  1 Peel two potatoes.

  6 Season with salt and pepper and serve.

  3 Put the cooked potatoes in a bowl with milk and butter, then mash.

  5 Add the onions to the mashed potatoes.

  2 Boil the potatoes until they are done.

47

Using Prior Knowledge: Greek and Roman Mythology

Directions: Before reading about Greek and Roman mythology in the following section, answer these questions.

1. Hercules is a man from Greek and Roman mythology. Write a short paragraph describing what you know about Hercules.

2. Can you think of anything today that derived its name from a Greek or Roman myth?

Answers will vary.

3. Compare and _____ what you know of Greek and Roman beliefs about mythology with your beliefs.

4. Many constellations are named after gods, goddesses and mythical creatures. Name at least six.

48

Comprehension: Roman Legends

Long ago, people did not know as much about science and astronomy as they do today. When they did not understand something, they thought the "gods" were responsible. The ancient Romans believed there were many gods and that each god or goddess (a female god) was responsible for certain things.

For example, the Romans believed Ceres (Sir-eez) was the goddess who made flowers, plants, trees and other things grow. She was a lot like what people today refer to as Mother Nature. Ceres was also responsible for the good weather that made crops grow. You can see why Ceres was such an important goddess to the ancient Romans.

Apollo was the god of the sun. People believed he used his chariot to pull the sun up each day and take it down at night. Apollo was extremely good-looking. His home was a golden palace near the sun surrounded by fluffy white clouds. Apollo had to work every single day, but he lived a wonderful life.

Jupiter was the most important god of all. He was the god who ruled all of the other gods, as well as the people. Jupiter was also called Jove. Maybe you have heard someone use the exclamation, "By Jove!" That person is talking about Jupiter! The word **father** is derived from the word **Jupiter**. Although he did not really exist, Jupiter influenced our language.

Directions: Answer these questions about Roman legends.

1. What imaginary figure is Ceres compared to today? **Mother Nature**

2. Where did Apollo live? **a golden palace near the sun**

3. The word **father** is derived from the name of this god:

  ☐ Ceres ☐ Apollo ☒ Jupiter

4. Which is not true of Apollo?

  ☐ He had to work every day.
  ☒ He lived in a mountain cave.
  ☐ He was very handsome.

49

Comprehension: Apollo and Phaethon

Apollo, the sun god, had a son named Phaethon (Fay-a-thun). Like most boys, Phaethon was proud of his father. He liked to brag to his friends about Apollo's important job, but no one believed that the great Apollo was his father.

Phaethon thought of a way to prove to his friends that he was telling the truth. He went to Apollo and asked if he could drive the chariot of the sun. If his friends saw him making the sun rise and set, they would be awestruck!

Apollo did not want to let Phaethon drive the chariot. He was afraid Phaethon was not strong enough to control the horses. But Phaethon begged until Apollo gave in. "Stay on the path," Apollo said. "If you dip too low, the sun will catch the earth on fire. If you go too high, people will freeze."

Unfortunately, Apollo's worst fears came true. Phaethon could not control the horses. He let them pull the chariot of the sun too close to the earth. To keep the earth from burning, Jupiter, father of the gods, sent a thunderbolt that hit Phaethon and knocked him from the driver's seat. When Phaethon let go of the reins, the horses pulled the chariot back up onto the proper path. Phaethon was killed as he fell to earth. His body caught fire and became a shooting star.

Directions: Answer these questions about the Roman legend of Apollo and his son.

1. Who did not believe Apollo was Phaethon's father? **Phaethon's friends**

2. What did Phaethon do to prove Apollo was his father? **drove the chariot of the sun**

3. Why did Jupiter send a lightning bolt? **to keep the earth from burning by knocking Phaethon from the driver's seat**

4. Which was not a warning from Apollo to Phaethon?

  ☐ Don't go too close to the earth. It will burn up.
  ☒ Don't pet the horses. They will run wild.
  ☐ Don't go too far from the earth. It will freeze.

50

Context Clues: Mighty Hercules

Some people lift weights to build their strength. But Hercules (Her-cu-lees) had a different idea. He carried a calf on his shoulders every day. As the calf grew, it got heavier, and Hercules got stronger. Eventually, Hercules could carry a full-grown bull!

Hercules used his enormous strength to do many kind things. He became famous. Even the king had heard of Hercules! He called for Hercules to kill a lion that had killed many people in his kingdom. Hercules tracked the lion to its den and strangled it. Then Hercules made clothes for himself from the lion's skin. This kind of apparel was unusual, and soon Hercules was recognized everywhere he went. Hercules was big and his clothes made it easy to pick him out in a crowd!

The king asked Hercules to stay in his kingdom and help protect the people who lived there. Hercules performed many feats of strength and bravery. He caught a golden deer for the king. The deer had outrun everyone else. Then Hercules killed a giant, a dragon and other dangerous creatures. Hercules became a hero and was known throughout the kingdom.

Directions: Answer these questions about Hercules.

1. Use context clues to choose the correct definition of **enormous**.

  ☒ huge ☐ tiny ☐ smart

2. Use context clues to choose the correct definition of **strangle**.

  ☐ beat ☒ choke ☐ tickle

3. Use context clues to choose the correct definition of **den**.

  ☐ pond ☐ hutch ☒ home

4. Use context clues to choose the correct definition of **apparel**.

  ☐ appearance ☒ clothing ☐ personality

5. Use context clues to choose the correct definition of **feat**.

  ☐ trick ☐ treat ☒ act

51

115

© 1999 American Education Publishing Co.

Comprehension: Ceres and Venus

Remember Ceres? She was like Mother Nature to the ancient Romans.

Ceres made the flowers, plants and trees grow. She made crops come up and rain fall. Ceres was a very important goddess. The ancient Romans depended on her for many things.

Although the gods and goddesses were important, they had faults like ordinary people. They argued with one another. Sometimes they got mad and lost their tempers. This is what happened to Ceres and another goddess named Venus (Veen-us). Venus, who was the goddess of love and beauty, got mad at Ceres. She decided to hurt Ceres by causing Pluto, gloomy god of the underworld, to fall in love with Ceres' daughter, Proserpine (Pro-sur-pin-ay).

To accomplish this, Venus sent her son Cupid to shoot Pluto with his bow and arrow. Venus told Cupid that the man shot by this arrow would then fall in love with the first woman he saw. Venus instructed Cupid to make sure that woman was Ceres' daughter. Cupid waited with his bow and arrow until Pluto drove by Ceres' garden in his chariot. In the garden was Proserpine. Just as Pluto's chariot got near her, Cupid shot his arrow.

Ping! The arrow hit Pluto. It did not hurt, but it did its job well. Pluto fell instantly in love with poor Proserpine, who was quietly planting flowers. Pluto was not a gentleman. He did not even introduce himself! Pluto swooped down and carried Proserpine off in his chariot before he could call for help.

Directions: Answer these questions about Ceres and Venus.

1. With whom was Venus angry? __Ceres__

2. How did Venus decide to get even? __She made Pluto fall in love with Ceres' daughter.__

3. Ceres' daughter's name was
☐ Perserpine. ☐ Prosperline. ☒ Proserpine.

4. Venus' son's name was
☐ Apollo. ☒ Cupid. ☐ Persperpine.

52

Comprehension: Proserpine and Pluto

Proserpine was terrified in Pluto's palace in the underworld. She missed her mother, Ceres, and would not stop crying.

When Ceres discovered her daughter was missing, she searched the whole Earth looking for her. Of course, she did not find her. Ceres was so unhappy about Proserpine's disappearance that she refused to do her job, which was to make things grow. When Ceres did not work, rain could not fall and crops could not grow. Finally, Ceres went to Jupiter for help.

Jupiter was powerful, but so was Pluto. Jupiter told Ceres he could get Proserpine back from Pluto if she had not eaten any of Pluto's food. As it turned out, Proserpine had eaten something. She had swallowed six seeds from a piece of fruit. Because he felt sorry for the people on Earth who were suffering, Pluto told Jupiter that Proserpine could return temporarily to Ceres so she would cheer up and make crops grow again. But Pluto later came back for Proserpine and forced her to spend six months each year with him in the underworld—one month for each seed she had eaten. Every time she returned to the underworld, Ceres mourned and refused to do her job. This is how the Romans explained the seasons—when Proserpine is on Earth with Ceres, it is spring and summer; when Proserpine goes to the underworld, it is fall and winter.

Directions: Answer these questions about Proserpine and Pluto.

1. What happened to Ceres when Pluto took her daughter? __She was very unhappy and refused to do her job.__

2. Whom did Ceres ask for help to get her daughter back? __Jupiter__

3. Why did Proserpine have to return to Pluto's underworld? __She had to spend one month there for each seed she had eaten.__

4. How long did Proserpine have to stay in the underworld each time she returned? __six months__

53

Comprehension: Orpheus Saves the Day

Orpheus (Or-fee-us) was a talented Greek musician. Once, by playing beautiful music on his lyre (ly-er), he caused a ship that was stuck in the sand to move into the water. (A lyre is a stringed instrument that looks like a small harp and fits in the musician's lap.) The song was about how wonderful it was to sail upon the sea. The ship itself must have thought the song was wonderful, too, because it slipped into the water and sailed away!

There was a reason the ship understood Orpheus' song. Inside the ship was a piece of wood that a goddess had given to the captain of the ship. The captain's name was Jason. Once, Jason had helped an old woman across a deep river. He later learned that the old woman was a goddess. To thank him, the goddess gave Jason a piece of wood that could talk. She told him to use the wood when he built a new ship. If he ever got stuck while building the ship and did not know what to do, the goddess told Jason to ask the wood.

Several times, Jason and his crew got instructions from the wood. Finally, the ship was finished. It was beautiful and very large. Because it was so big, Jason and his men were unable to move it into the water. They called on Hercules for help, and even he could not make it budge. That's when Orpheus saved the day with his lyre.

Directions: Answer these questions about Orpheus' amazing talent.

1. Who owned the ship that was stuck? __Jason__

2. Where was the ship stuck? __in the sand__

3. Why did the ship get stuck? __It was too large to move.__

4. A lyre looks like what other instrument?
☐ harmonica ☐ guitar ☒ harp

5. Who did Jason first ask for help to move the ship?
☐ Orpheus ☒ Hercules ☐ Jupiter

54

Recalling Details: Centaurs and Minotaurs

Directions: Read the story below about the strange imaginary creatures in Greek mythology called centaurs and minotaurs. Then complete the puzzle.

Besides the gods, there were other powerful creatures in Greek mythology. Among them were minotaurs and centaurs. A minotaur (min-oh-tar) was half man and half bull. A centaur (sen-tar) was half man and half horse. Centaurs were said to live in the mountains near an area of Greece called Thessaly. Minotaurs were said to live in the underworld.

Across:
3. Centaurs were said to live near this area of Greece.
5. A creature that lived in the underworld
7. Minotaurs lived here.

Down:
1. A creature that is half horse
2. Some creatures in Greek mythology were half beast and half _____.
4. Back end of a centaur
5. Another word for Greek stories
6. Back end of a minotaur

55

Review

Directions: Read the paragraph below. Then circle the answers to the questions in the word search.

Do you remember how Roman and Greek myths came about? People used myths about gods, goddesses and strange creatures to explain why certain things happened. If no rain fell, it was because Ceres was angry. If someone was hit by lightning, it was because that person had angered Jupiter. If a marriage did not work out, Venus or her son Cupid were to blame. If people were wicked, Pluto must have had a hand in their transgressions.

1. Which god or goddess was responsible if no rain fell? __Ceres__

2. Which god or goddess was responsible if someone was hit by lightning? __Jupiter__

3. Which god or goddess was responsible if a marriage failed? __Venus or Cupid__

4. Which god or goddess was responsible if people were wicked? __Pluto__

5. Choose the correct definition of **transgressions**.
☐ happiness ☒ sins ☐ conditions

```
V  A  D  C  E  R  E  S
W  P  M  U  L  A  R  I
Q  L  A  P  K  B  C  N
J  U  P  I  T  E  R  S
L  T  K  D  A  J  D  I
Y  O  S  U  N  E  V  O
```

56

Review

Directions: Follow the instructions below.

1. Define the following words from this section.

astronomy: _____

reins: _____

lyre: _____

centaur: _____

minotaur: _____

myth: _____

2. Choose two words from
1) __Answers will vary.__
2)

3. Write a summary of the selection "Mighty Hercules" (page 51).

_____
_____
_____

4. Complete the sequence of events from the selection "Proserpine and Pluto" (page 53).
1) Pluto fell in love with Proserpine and kidnapped her in his chariot.
2) _____
3) _____
4) _____
5) _____

57

© 1999 American Education Publishing Co.   **116**

Using Prior Knowledge: Art

Directions: Before reading about art in the following section, answer these questions.

1. Write a short paragraph about a famous artist of your choice.

2. Many artists paint realistic scenes. Other artists paint imaginary scenes. Which do you prefer? Why?

3. Although we often think ~~~~ pture, fabric weavings ar ~~~~ what type? If not, wh ~~~~

Answers will vary.

4. Why are art museums important to society?

5. Why do you think some artwork is worth so much money? Would you pay several thousand dollars for a piece of artwork? Why or why not?

58

Main Idea: Creating Art

No one knows exactly when the first human created the first painting. Crude drawings and paintings on the walls of caves show that humans have probably always expressed themselves through art. These early cave pictures show animals being hunted, people dancing and other events of daily life. The simplicity of the paintings reflect the simple lifestyles of these primitive people.

The subjects of early paintings also help to make another important point. Art is not created out of nothing. The subjects an artist chooses to paint reflect the history, politics and culture of the time and place in which he/she lives. An artist born and raised in New York City, for example, is not likely to paint scenes of the Rocky Mountains. An artist living in the Rockies is not likely to paint pictures of city life.

Of course, not all paintings are realistic. Many artists choose to paint pictures that show their own "inner vision" as opposed to what they see with their eyes. Many religious paintings of earlier centuries look realistic but contain figures of angels. These paintings combine the artist's inner vision of angels with other things, such as church buildings, that can be seen.

Directions: Answer these questions about creating art.

1. Circle the main idea:

Art was important to primitive people because it showed hunting and dancing scenes, and is still important today.

Through the ages, artists have created paintings that reflect the culture, history and politics of the times, as well as their own inner visions.

2. Why is an artist living in the Rocky Mountains less likely to paint city scenes?

Artists usually portray something that is part of their lives.

3. In addition to what they see with their eyes, what do some artists' paintings also show?

their inner feelings or visions

59

Comprehension: Leonardo da Vinci

Many people believe that Leonardo da Vinci, an Italian artist and inventor who lived from 1452 to 1519, was the most brilliant person ever born. He was certainly a man ahead of his time! Records show that da Vinci loved the earth and was curious about everything on it.

To learn about the human body, he dissected corpses to find out what was inside. In the 15th and 16th centuries, dissecting the dead was against the laws of the Catholic church. Leonardo was a brave man!

He was also an inventor. Leonardo invented a parachute and designed a type of helicopter—5 centuries before airplanes were invented! Another of da Vinci's major talents was painting. You have probably seen a print, or copy, of one of his most famous paintings. It is called *The Last Supper*, and shows Jesus eating his final meal with his disciples. It took da Vinci 3 years to paint *The Last Supper*. The man who hired da Vinci to do the painting was upset. He went to da Vinci to ask why it was taking so long. The problem, said da Vinci, was that in the painting, Jesus has just told the disciples that one of them would betray him. He wanted to get their expressions exactly right as each cried out, "Lord, am I the one?"

Another famous painting by da Vinci is called the *Mona Lisa*. Have you seen a print of this painting? Maybe you have been lucky enough to see the original hanging in a Paris art museum called the Louvre (Loov). If so, you know that Mona Lisa has a wistful expression on her face. The painting is a real woman, the wife of an Italian merchant. Art historians believe she looks wistful because one of her children had recently died.

Directions: Answer these questions about Leonardo da Vinci.

1. How old was da Vinci when he died? _67_

2. Name two of da Vinci's inventions. _parachute and helicopter_

3. Name two famous paintings by da Vinci. _Mona Lisa, The Last Supper_

4. In which Paris museum does *Mona Lisa* hang? ☐ Lourre ☐ Loure ☒ Louvre

60

Context Clues: Leonardo da Vinci

Directions: Read the sentences below. Use context clues to figure out the meaning of the bold words.

1. Some people are **perplexed** when they look at *The Last Supper*, but others understand it immediately.
   ☐ unhappy ☐ happy ☒ puzzled

2. Because his model felt **melancholy** about the death of her child, da Vinci had music played to lift her spirits as she painted the *Mona Lisa*.
   ☒ sad ☐ unfriendly ☐ hostile

3. Because da Vinci's work is so famous, many people **erroneously** assume that he left behind many paintings. In fact, he left only 20.
   ☐ rightly ☐ correctly ☒ wrongly

4. Leonardo da Vinci was not like most other people. He didn't care what others thought of him—he led an interesting and **unconventional** life.
   ☐ dull ☒ not ordinary ☐ ordinary

5. The **composition** of *The Last Supper* is superb. All the parts of the painting seem to fit together beautifully.
   ☐ the picture frame ☒ parts of the picture

6. Leonardo's **genius** set him apart from people with ordinary minds. He never married, he had few friends and he spent much of his time alone.
   ☒ great mental abilities ☐ great physical abilities
   ☐ improper way to do things ☐ great way to do things

7. Because he was a loner, da Vinci worried no one would come to his funeral when he died. In his will, he set aside 70 cents each to hire 60 **mourners** to accompany his body to his grave.
   ☐ friends ☒ people who grieve ☐ people who smile

61

Comprehension: Michelangelo

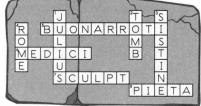

Another famous painter of the late 14th and early 15th centuries was Michelangelo Buonarroti. Michelangelo, who lived from 1475 to 1564, was also an Italian. Like da Vinci, his genius was apparent at a young age. When he was 13, the ruler of his hometown of Florence, Lorenzo Medici (Muh-dee-chee), befriended Michelangelo and asked him to live in the palace. There Michelangelo studied sculpture and met many artists.

By the time he was 18, Michelangelo was a respected sculptor. He created one of his most famous religious sculptures, the *Pieta* (pee-ay-tah), when he was only 21. Then the Medici family abruptly fell from power and Michelangelo had to leave Florence.

Still, his work was well known and he was able to make a living. In 1503, Pope Julius II called Michelangelo to Rome. He wanted Michelangelo to paint the tomb where he would someday be buried. Michelangelo preferred sculpting to painting, but no one turned down the pope! Before Michelangelo finished his painting, however, the pope ordered Michelangelo to begin painting the ceiling of the Sistine Chapel inside the Vatican. (The Vatican is the palace and surrounding area where the pope lives in Rome.)

Michelangelo was very angry! He did not like to paint. He wanted to create sculptures. But no one turns down the pope. After much complaining, Michelangelo began work on what would be his most famous project.

Directions: Answer these questions about Michelangelo.

1. How old was Michelangelo when he died? _89_

2. What was the first project Pope Julius II asked Michelangelo to paint?
   his tomb

3. What is the Vatican? _palace and grounds where the Pope lives_

4. What was the second project the pope asked Michelangelo to do?
   ☐ paint his tomb's ceiling ☒ paint the Sistine Chapel's ceiling

62

Recalling Details: Michelangelo Puzzler

Directions: Use the facts you learned about Michelangelo to complete the puzzle.

Crossword:
- ROME
- BUONARROTI
- TOMB
- SISTINE
- MEDICI
- SCULPT
- PIETA

Across:
5. Michelangelo's last name
6. Name of the family who asked Michelangelo to live in the palace
7. Michelangelo like to ____ more than paint.
8. The religious sculpture he created at age 21

Down:
1. The name of the pope who asked Michelangelo to paint
2. The first thing the pope asked Michelangelo to paint
3. The name of the chapel in the Vatican
4. The city in which the Vatican is located

63

117

Comprehension: Rembrandt

Most art critics agree that Rembrandt (Rem-brant) was one of the greatest painters of all time. This Dutch artist, who lived from 1606 to 1669, painted some of the world's finest portraits.

Rembrandt, whose full name was Rembrandt van Rijn, was born in Holland to a wealthy family. He was sent to a fine university, but he did not like his studies. He only wanted to paint. He sketched the faces of people around him. During his lifetime, Rembrandt painted 11 portraits of his father and nearly as many of his mother. From the beginning, the faces of old people fascinated him.

When he was 25, Rembrandt went to paint in Amsterdam, a large city in Holland where he lived for the rest of his life. There he married a wealthy woman named Saskia, whom he loved deeply. She died from a disease called tuberculosis (ta-bur-ku-lo-sis) after only 8 years, leaving behind a young son named Titus (Ty-tuss).

Rembrandt was heartbroken over his wife's death. He began to spend all his time painting. But instead of painting what his customers wanted, he painted exactly the way he wanted. Unsold pictures filled his house. They were wonderful paintings, but they were not the type of portraits people wanted. Rembrandt could not pay his debts. He and his son were thrown into the streets. The creditors took his home, his possessions and his paintings. One of the finest painters on Earth was treated like a criminal.

Directions: Answer these questions about Rembrandt.

1. How old was Rembrandt when he died? __63__

2. In what city did he spend most of his life? __Amsterdam__

3. How many children did Rembrandt have? __one__

4. Rembrandt's wife was named

☐ Sasha.   ☒ Saskia.   ☐ Saksia.

5. These filled his house after his wife's death.

☐ friends   ☐ customers   ☒ unsold paintings

64

Recalling Details: Rembrandt Puzzler

Directions: Use the facts you learned about Rembrandt to complete the puzzle.

Crossword answers:
AMSTERDAM
TUBER / FATHER
EIGHT
DEBTS / CUSTOMERS
TITUS
OLD
SASKIA

Across:

1. City Rembrandt went to when he was 25

5. Number of years Rembrandt was married

6. These people did not like Rembrandt's paintings.

7. Rembrandt named his son ____.

8. Age group of people Rembrandt liked to paint most

9. Rembrandt had a wife named ____.

Down:

2. The disease from which Rembrandt's wife died

3. Man Rembrandt painted in 11 portraits

4. Rembrandt was thrown out of his house because he could not pay these.

65

Comprehension: More About Rembrandt

The people who took Rembrandt's home and possessions left behind something very important. They left his blank canvases and art tools. Also, his housekeeper had hidden a few of his paintings. After he was thrown out of his home, Rembrandt was able to sell the paintings. He moved to a poor neighborhood with his son and housekeeper and began painting again.

For the rest of his life, Rembrandt painted dark paintings. The colors he used included grays, browns and blacks, with a rich yellow color used for contrast. Rembrandt could use dark colors better than any other painter. He painted 145 religious pictures and 650 drawings of subjects from the Bible. If you have ever seen a painting or sketch by Rembrandt, you know that his work seems to portray not just people's faces but their souls as well.

Directions: Answer these questions about Rembrandt.

1. Circle the main idea:

Rembrandt was not defeated when his home and possessions were taken from him. He continued to paint extraordinary pictures.

Rembrandt had an unfortunate life and he never got over the treatment he received at the hands of his creditors.

2. Explain how to identify Rembrandt's paintings through the colors he used.

__Rembrandt used dark grays, browns and blacks with a rich yellow for contrast.__

3. Choose the correct definition of **sketch**.

☐ cartoon   ☒ drawing   ☐ poem

4. How many religious paintings and drawings from the Bible did Rembrandt create?

__145 paintings and 650 drawings__

5. What is remarkable about Rembrandt's portraits? __They seem to portray not only people's faces but also their souls.__

66

Review

Directions: Follow the instructions below.

1. Write a one-sentence main idea for the selection "Leonardo da Vinci" (page 60).

2. Write a summary of the selection "Leonardo da Vinci" (page 60).

3. Complete the sequence of events from the selection "Michelangelo" (page 62).

1) Michelang...

2)

3)   Answers will vary.

4)

5)

6)

7)

4. Define the following words from this section.

crude: _____

dissect: _____

disciples: _____

merchant: _____

wistful: _____

67

Using Prior Knowledge: Stamp Collecting

Directions: Before reading about stamp collecting in the following section, answer these questions.

1. Why do you think people collect stamps?

2. What hobby do you most enjoy? Why?

3. Name at le...   Answers will vary.

4. Why do you think the postal service issues many different stamps each year? Why not just issue one stamp?

5. The postal service recently introduced self-stick stamps. What are the benefits of these stamps? Do you think these create any drawbacks for collectors?

68

Fact or Opinion?

Directions: Read the paragraphs below. Then, in the corresponding numbered blanks, write whether each numbered sentence is a fact or an opinion.

(1) An important rule for stamp collectors to follow is never to handle stamps with their fingers. (2) Instead, to keep the stamps clean, collectors use stamp tongs to pick up stamps. (3) Stamps are stored by being placed on mounts. (4) Stamp mounts are plastic holders that fit around the stamp and keep it clean. (5) The backs of the mounts are sticky, so they can be stuck onto a stamp album page. (6) What a great idea!

(7) The stamps are mounted in stamp albums that have either white or black pages. (8) Some people prefer black pages, claiming that the stamps "show" better. (9) Some people prefer white pages, claiming that they give the album a cleaner look. (10) I think this foolish bickering over page colors is ridiculous!

1. __fact__

2. __fact__

3. __fact__

4. __fact__

5. __fact__

6. __opinion__

7. __fact__

8. __opinion__

9. __opinion__

10. __opinion__

69

Comprehension: More Stamp Collecting

Many people collect stamps in blocks of four. Each stamp in the block is stuck to the other stamps along the edges. Collectors do not tear the stamps apart from one another. They buy blocks of stamps bearing new designs directly from the post office. Then they mount the blocks of stamps and place them in their albums.

Collectors also get their stamps off of envelopes. This is a bit tricky, because the stamps are glued on. Usually, collectors soak the stamps in warm water to loosen the glue. Then they gently pull the stamps from the paper and let them dry before mounting them.

Some beginners start their collections by buying a packet of mixed stamps. The packets, or bags, contain a variety of different stamps. Beginners buy these packets from companies that supply stamps to philatelists (fuh-lay-tell-lists). Philately (fuh-lay-tel-lee) is the collection and study of postage stamps. Philatelists are the people who collect and study them.

Packets of stamps usually contain stamps from many different countries. Often, they contain duplicates of some of the stamps. Suppliers usually don't sort the stamps that go into the packets for beginners. They leave that for beginning philatelists to enjoy!

Directions: Answer these questions about stamp collecting.

1. Name three places some people get stamps. **post office, old envelopes and buy them**

2. What is the word that describes the collection and study of stamps? **philately**

3. What are people called who collect and study stamps? **philatelists**

4. The bag that a mixture of stamps comes in is called a

☐ postal bag. ☒ packet. ☐ philatelist.

5. Do stamp mixtures usually include only U.S. stamps?

☐ Yes ☒ No

70

Recalling Details: Philately Abbreviations

Like other hobbies, philately has its own jargon and symbols. Collectors and dealers know what they mean, but "outsiders" would be puzzled if they saw the following abbreviations without their definitions. Read them carefully, then refer to them when answering the questions below.

Avg. — average condition	**M** — mint (excellent and unused) condition
blk. — block of four stamps	**s** — single stamp
C — cancelled (used) stamp	**U** — used stamp
OG — original gum	**VF** — very fine condition
(glue on back of stamp)	**Wmk** — watermark (can occur when water
G — good condition	is used to remove stamp from envelope)

Directions: Answer these questions about the abbreviations used by stamp dealers and collectors.

1. If a philatelist wrote the following description, what would he/she mean?
I have a blk. in VF. **I have a block of four stamps in very fine conditions.**

2. What does this mean? **s with OG, condition M** **single stamp with the original gum on the back in excellent and unused condition**

3. What other abbreviation would most likely be used do describe a used (U) stamp? **C (cancelled)**

4. What does this mean? **s in Avg. with Wmk** **a single stamp in average condition with a watermark**

5. Which is more valuable, a rare stamp in **M** or **VF** condition? **M (mint)**

6. Would you rather own a single U stamp or a blk. in M? **a blk. in M**

71

Comprehension: Faces on Stamps

If anyone ever tries to sell you a stamp with a picture of former Vice President Dan Quayle on it, just say no! In the United States, only people who have died can have their pictures on stamps. That is why the singer Elvis Presley's face appeared on stamps only after he died.

Many U.S. presidents' faces have been on postage stamps, as have pictures of the faces of other important people in U.S. history. Some people's faces have been on many different stamps. Through the years, George Washington and Benjamin Franklin have been on dozens of different types of stamps!

Other people whose pictures have been on stamps include John Quincy Adams, the sixth president of the United States; Jane Addams, a U.S. social worker and writer; Louisa May Alcott, author of *Little Women* and many other books; Clara Barton, nurse and founder of the American Red Cross; Alexander Graham Bell, inventor of the telephone; and poet Emily Dickinson. These are only a few of the hundreds of famous Americans whose faces have appeared on U.S. postage stamps.

Directions: Answer these questions about some of the people whose faces have appeared on U.S. stamps.

1. Name six occupations of people whose faces have appeared on postage stamps. **president, writer, entertainer, nurse, inventor, social worker**

2. What two people's pictures have appeared on more stamps than any others? **George Washington, Benjamin Franklin**

3. Why can't Dan Quayle's face appear on a postage stamp? **He is still alive and people must be dead to appear on a U.S. stamp.**

4. Which person featured on a postage stamp was a social worker?

☐ Clara Barton ☐ Louisa May Alcott ☒ Jane Addams

5. Which person featured on a postage stamp was an inventor?

☐ Emily Dickinson ☒ Alexander Graham Bell ☐ John Quincy Adams

72

Recalling Details: Postage Stamp Puzzler

Directions: Use the facts you learned about the faces on postage stamps to complete the puzzle. (There is no space between answers that have more than two words.)

Across:

2. Occupation of Alexander Graham Bell, whose face is on a stamp
6. Famous singer whose face appears on stamps
7. This living politician can't be on a stamp (last name only).

Down:

1. Along with Washington, he's appeared on the most stamps.
3. Occupation of Clara Barton, whose face is on a stamp
4. Can President Clinton be on a stamp?
5. Occupation of Emily Dickinson, whose face is on a stamp

73

Comprehension: Valuable Stamps

Most people collect stamps as a hobby. They spend small sums of money to get the stamps they want, or they trade stamps with other collectors. They rarely make what could be considered "big money" from their philately hobby.

A few collectors are in the business of philately as opposed to the hobby. To the people who can afford it, some stamps are worth big money. For example, a U.S. airmail stamp with a face value of 24 cents when it was issued in 1918 is now worth more than $35,000 if a certain design appears on the stamp. Another stamp, the British Guiana, an ugly stamp that cost only a penny when it was issued, later sold for $280,000!

The Graf Zeppelin is another example of an ugly stamp that became valuable. Graf Zeppelin is the name of a type of airship, similar to what we now call a "blimp," invented around the turn of the century. Stamps were issued to mark the first roundtrip flight of the Zeppelin made between two continents. A set of three of these stamps cost $4.55 when they were issued. The stamps were ugly and few of them sold. The postal service destroyed the rest. Now, because they are rare, each set of the Graf Zeppelin stamps is worth hundreds of dollars.

Directions: Answer these questions about valuable stamps.

1. What is the most valuable stamp described? **the British Guiana**

2. For how much did this stamp originally sell? **one penny**

3. What did a collector later pay for it? **$280,000**

4. The Graf Zeppelin stamps originally sold for $4.55 for a set of

☐ four. ☐ six. ☒ three.

5. Which stamp did the postal service destroy because it didn't sell?

☐ British Guiana ☒ Graf Zeppelin ☐ British Zeppelin

74

Fact or Opinion?

Directions: Read the paragraphs below. Then, in the corresponding numbered blanks, write whether each numbered sentence is a fact or an opinion.

(1) Nearly every valuable stamp on Earth has been counterfeited (coun-ter-fit-tid) at one time or another. (2) A "counterfeit" is a fake that looks nearly identical to the original. (3) It takes a lot of nerve to try to pass off counterfeits as the real thing. (4) Counterfeiting is big business, especially with stamps from overseas. (5) Because a collector often has no original for comparison, he/she can be easily fooled by a good counterfeit!

(6) One way people can make sure a stamp is real is to have it checked by a company that authenticates (aw-then-fi-kates) stamps. (7) To "authenticate" means to prove the stamp is real. (8) Of course, there is a fee for this service. (9) But I think paying a reasonable fee is worth what collectors get in return. (10) Those counterfeiters should be locked up forever!

1. **fact**
2. **fact**
3. **opinion**
4. **fact**
5. **fact**
6. **fact**
7. **fact**
8. **fact**
9. **opinion**
10. **opinion**

75

119

Comprehension: Stamp Value

It's nearly impossible to predict which stamps will rise in value. Why? Because the value is based on the law of supply and demand. How much does someone or a group of "someones" want for a particular stamp? If many people want a stamp, the value will increase, especially if few of the stamps exist.

However, collectors are also always on the lookout for things that can lower the value of a stamp. Are the stamp's perforations (per-four-ay-shuns) torn along the edges? (Perforations are ragged edges where stamps tear apart.) Is there a watermark on the stamp? Has the gum worn off the back? All these things can make a stamp less valuable.

Directions: Answer these questions about determining the value of stamps.

1. Name three things that can lower the value of a stamp.
   a watermark, the gum is worn off the back, the perforations are torn

2. Collecting stamps is a fascinating hobby.   Fact   (Opinion)

3. What is one thing the value of stamps is based upon? supply and demand

4. What will happen if many people want a rare stamp? The value will increase.

5. Explain how to spot a stamp that will become valuable. It would be very difficult to predict future value. It depends on these variables—how many people want to own it and how many stamps are available.

76

Review

Directions: Follow the instructions below.

1. Define the following words from this section.

   mount: _____
   bickering: _____
   philately: _____
   counterfeit: _____
   authenticate: _____
   perforations: _____

2. Choose two d   Answers will vary.
   1) _____
   2) _____

3. Write a one-sentence main idea for the selection "Stamp Value" (page 76).
   _____

4. Write a summary of the selection "Faces on Stamps" (page 72).
   _____

5. Write a summary of the selection "More About Stamp Collecting" (page 70).
   _____

77

Using Prior Knowledge: Writing

Directions: Before reading about writing in the following section, answer these questions.

1. What are some of the benefits of writing for young people?
   _____

2. What are some of the disadvantages of writing for young people?
   Answers will vary.

3. What type of _____

4. Why might it be difficult for a young person your age to publish his/her work?
   _____

5. On another sheet of paper, write a short journal entry describing how you feel about writing. Discuss whether you enjoy writing poetry, fiction, nonfiction, letters, and so on; if you find writing difficult or easy; and when and where you feel most comfortable writing.

78

Comprehension: Calling Young Poets and Writers!

Do you like to write poetry, short stories or articles? If so, you will be glad to learn that there are magazines dedicated to publishing children's writing.

Shoe Tree is a magazine for children ages 6 to 14. It's published three times a year by the National Association for Young Writers. Fictional stories, articles, poems, book reviews and humorous essays are all published in Shoe Tree. The magazine is headquartered at 215 Valle del Sol Drive, Santa Fe, New Mexico 87501.

Another magazine that publishes children's writing is Stone Soup. Stone Soup is published by the Children's Art Foundation, Box 83, Santa Cruz, California 95063. Stone Soup publishes poetry, science fiction, fiction and personal experience essays. This magazine also publishes drawings by children. Stone Soup publishes the work of children up to age 13.

A literary journal for young people is Writes of Passage: The Literary Journal for Teenagers. Writes of Passage is published by Writes of Passage USA, Inc., P.O. Box 1935, Livingston, New Jersey 07039. Writes of Passage accepts poems and short stories written by teens between 12 and 19.

Like all professional publications, Shoe Tree, Stone Soup and Writes of Passage want work that is spelled and punctuated correctly. Typed papers are preferred, but Shoe Tree will accept handwritten stories and poems that are clearly readable.

Directions: Answer these questions about magazines that publish children's writing.

1. In which publication can 15 year olds be published? Writes of Passage

2. If you are 14, you are too old to write for which magazine? Stone Soup

3. Which publication is published in Santa Fe? Shoe Tree

4. Which publication will accept handwritten stories?
   ☒ Shoe Tree   ☐ Stone Soup   ☐ Writes of Passage

79

Comprehension: Poems for Kids of All Ages

You're never too young or too old to appreciate poetry! Each year, many books of poems are published for children of all ages. The following books were published in 1990.

Nursery Poems and Prayers and Nursery Songs and Lullabies are books for very young children. Older kids will enjoy reading these books, also. You may remember a parent reading some of these poems to you when you were a small child. The author of both books is Bessie Pease Gutmann. The books are published by a company called Grosset & Dunlap.

If you like silly poems and riddles, you may enjoy My Head Is Red and Other Riddle Rhymes. The author is Myra Cohn Livingston. The publisher is Holiday House. The book contains 27 riddle poems for children ages 6 to 9.

A book of poems for children age 12 and older is Life Doesn't Frighten Me at All. The poems were compiled by John Agard. "Compiled by" means that Mr. Agard collected the poems from other places. He did not write the poems himself. The poems in Life Doesn't Frighten Me at All are about growing up, families and politics. The publisher is Henry Holt.

Directions: Answer these questions about the four poetry books.

1. What company published Nursery Songs and Lullabies? Grosset & Dunlap

2. Who is the author of Nursery Poems and Prayers?
   Bessie Pease Gutmann

3. Who is the author of My Head Is Red and Other Riddle Rhymes?
   Myra Cohn Livingston

4. Which book is for children age 12 and older? Life Doesn't Frighten Me at All

5. Who compiled the poems in Life Doesn't Frighten Me at All? John Agard

6. Which book is for children ages 6 to 9? My Head Is Red and Other Riddle Rhymes

7. Where were all these books published? Grosset & Dunlop, Holiday House, Henry Holt

80

Comprehension: *Highlights for Children*

Young writers today are lucky to have many magazines interested in publishing their work. Just as farmers take pigs and cows to markets to sell them, writers also have markets. Writers' markets are the magazines and newspapers that publish the things they write.

An excellent market for children's writing is Highlights for Children. Highlights is published at 803 Church Street, Honesdale, Pennsylvania 18431. A young writer who is published in this magazine will have many people read his/her work. Highlights has a circulation of more than 2 million! This means more than 2 million copies are printed and mailed each month to people who pay to receive it. Those people are called "subscribers."

About 20 percent of Highlights is written by children. Young writers up to age 15 can submit poetry, articles, jokes, riddles and pictures. Besides these opportunities for young writers, Highlights sponsors a fiction contest each year. Stories for the fiction contest should be no longer than 900 words. The type of fiction young writers are invited to submit changes each year.

In 1990, for example, Highlights editors asked young writers to send them humorous fiction. The deadline for the fiction contest is usually very early in the year. A "deadline" is the date by which a writer's work must be received by the publisher. Writing submitted after a deadline will not be considered for publication. Information about the annual fiction contest is printed in the fall issue of Highlights.

Directions: Answer these questions about Highlights magazine.

1. What are writers' markets? magazines and newspapers that publish young writer's material

2. What does "circulation" mean? the number of copies that are published and mailed

3. What is a subscriber? person who pays to recieve a publication

4. Highlights is published in
   ☐ New York City.   ☒ Honesdale, Pennsylvania.

5. Highlights accepts writing from children up to age
   ☐ 13.   ☐ 14.   ☒ 15.

81

Sequencing: Studying the Market

The writing of many talented young authors is often rejected because they send their work to the wrong type of magazine. For example, a beautiful poem sent to the editor of a magazine that publishes only science fiction is bound to be rejected. "Rejecting" a piece of writing means the editor does not want to print it in the magazine.

A sensible way to cut down the number of times a piece of writing is rejected is to first study the market. Remember, writers' markets are the magazines and newspapers that publish the things they write. "Studying" a particular market simply means that you should carefully read a copy of the magazine you would like to be published in.

Knowing the type of writing a magazine publishes will help you "target" your market. "Targeting" simply means picking out a magazine that publishes your type of writing. If you study the markets, then target them, you will send your beautiful poem only to magazines that publish poetry.

It is a good idea to check your work to see if it meets the needs of the magazines you have targeted. Is it too long or too short compared to other poems or stories printed in the magazine? Is the content too difficult or too easy? Revise your writing, if necessary. Then write a short letter to the editor, telling briefly about what you have written. Remember to include your home address and phone number in a large envelope, put what you have written, the letter, and a self-addressed, stamped envelope for the editor's reply.

Directions: Number in order the steps to take before submitting a piece of writing to an editor.

_7_ Mail what you have written to the editor.

_1_ Get several magazines for young writers.

_5_ Write a short letter to the editor about your work.

_3_ Target the magazines that might publish your type of writing.

_2_ Study the magazines to find out the type of writing they publish.

_4_ Check and revise your piece of writing, if necessary.

_6_ Include a stamped, self-addressed envelope with your writing.

82

Comprehension: "The Trains"

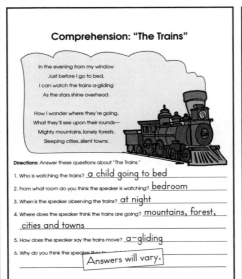

In the evening from my window
Just before I go to bed,
I can watch the trains a-gliding
As the stars shine overhead.

How I wonder where they're going,
What they'll see upon their rounds—
Mighty mountains, lonely forests,
Sleeping cities, silent towns.

Directions: Answer these questions about "The Trains."

1. Who is watching the trains? _a child going to bed_

2. From what room do you think the speaker is watching? _bedroom_

3. When is the speaker observing the trains? _at night_

4. Where does the speaker think the trains are going? _mountains, forest, cities and towns_

5. How does the speaker say the trains move? _a-gliding_

6. Why do you think the speaker likes to watch the trains? _Answers will vary._

83

Comprehension/Sequencing: Limericks

Limericks (lim-riks) are five-line poems that tend to be silly. The last word in certain lines of a limerick rhyme with the last word in other lines. This is called the poem's rhyme scheme. Usually, each line of a limerick has five to eight syllables. Here is a silly limerick. Can you use it as an example to write a limerick of your own?

There once was a girl from Hong Kong
Whose hair was abnormally long.
When she sat on the couch,
She always yelled, "Ouch!"
Then screamed that her hair was all wrong!

Directions: Answer these questions about limericks.

1. Which lines rhyme in the rhyme scheme of the limerick above?
1, 2 & 5 and 3 & 4

2. Number in order the events in the limerick.

_4_ The girl screamed that her hair was all wrong.

_1_ The girl grew her hair too long.

_3_ The girl yelled, "Ouch!"

_2_ The girl sat on the couch.

3. How many syllables does line one in the limerick have? _8_

4. How many syllables does line three in the limerick have? _6_

5. Why is the girl's hair "all wrong"? _she sat on it and pulled it_

6. What does "rhyme scheme" mean? _The last word in certain lines rhyme with the last word in other lines._

84

Review

Directions: Follow the instructions below.

1. Summarize the message of the poem "The Trains."

Answers will vary.

2. List four publications that publish young people's work.

Shoe Tree   _Stone Soup_

Wombat   _Highlights_

3. Why is it important to revise and edit your work several times?

4. Write a one-sentence main idea for the selection "Highlights for Children" (page 81).

5. Write a summary of the selection "Studying the Market."

Answers will vary.

6. Write a silly limerick of your own below.

85

Using Prior Knowledge: Big Cats

Directions: Before reading about big cats in the following section, answer these questions.

1. Name at least four big wild cats.

2. Compare and contrast a house cat with a wild cat.

3. What impact _____ on big cats?   _Answers will vary._

4. Do you have a cat? What are the special qualities of this pet? Write about your cat's name and its personality traits. If you don't have a cat, write about a cat you would like to have.

86

Comprehension: Jaguars

The jaguar is a large cat, standing up to 2 feet tall at the shoulder. Its body can reach 73 inches long, and the tail can be another 30 inches long. The jaguar is characterized by its yellowish-red coat covered with black spots. The spots themselves are made up of a central spot surrounded by a circle of spots.

Jaguars are not known to attack humans, but some ranchers claim that jaguars attack their cattle. This claim has given jaguars a bad reputation.

The jaguar can be found in southern North America, but is most populous in Central and South America. Jaguars are capable climbers and swimmers, and they eat a wide range of animals.

Female jaguars have between one and four cubs after a gestation of 93 to 105 days. Cubs stay with the mother for 2 years. Jaguars are known to have a life expectancy of at least 22 years.

Directions: Use context clues for these definitions.

1. populous: _____

2. reputation: _____   _Answers will vary._

3. gestation: _____

Directions: Answer these questions about jaguars.

4. Describe the spots on a jaguar's coat.
a central spot surrounded by a circle of spots

5. Why would it be to a jaguar's advantage to have spots on its coat?
Answers will vary.

87

121

Comprehension: Leopards

The leopard is a talented nocturnal hunter and can see very well in the dark. Because of its excellent climbing ability, the leopard is able to stalk and kill monkeys and baboons. Leopards are also known to consume mice, porcupines and fruit. Although the true leopard is characterized by a light beige coat with black spots, some leopards can be entirely black. These leopards are called black panthers. Many people refer to other cat species as leopards. Cheetahs are sometimes referred to as hunting leopards. The clouded leopard lives in southeastern Asia and has a grayish spotted coat. The snow leopard, which has a white coat, lives in Central Asia.

A leopard's spots help to camouflage (cam-o-flo) it as it hunts.

True leopards can grow to over 6 feet long, not including their 3-foot-long tail. Leopards can be found in Africa and Asia.

Directions: Use context clues for these definitions.

1. consume: _____
2. ability: _____ *Answers will vary.*
3. nocturnal: _____

Directions: Answer these questions about leopards.

4. List three differences between the leopard and the jaguar.
1. Leopards live in Africa and Asia, while jaguars live in Central and South America.
2. Leopards are light beige with black spots; jaguars are yellowish-red with black spots.
3. Leopards have black spots; jaguars have a central spot surrounded by a circle of spots.

5. What makes a leopard able to hunt monkeys and baboons?
It has excellent climbing ability.

88

Comprehension: Lynxes

Lynxes are strange-looking cats with very long legs and large paws. Their bodies are a mere 51 inches in length, and they have short little tails. Most lynxes have a clump of hair that extends past the tip of their ears.

Lynxes not only are known to chase down their prey, but also to leap on them from a perch above the ground. They eat small mammals and birds, as well as an occasional deer.

There are four types of lynxes. Bobcats can be found in all areas of the United States except the Midwest. The Spanish lynx is an endangered species. The Eurasian lynx, also known as the northern lynx, and the Canadian lynx are two other kinds of lynxes.

Directions: Use context clues for these definitions.

1. prey: _____
2. perch: _____ *Answers will vary.*

Directions: Answer these questions about lynxes.

3. What are the four types of lynxes? bobcats, Spanish lynx, Eurasian lynx, Canadian lynx

4. Use the following words in a sentence of your own.
mammal _____
endangered _____ *Answers will vary.*

5. Do you believe it is important to classify animals as "endangered" to protect a species that is low in population? Explain your answer.
_____ *Answers will vary.*

89

Comprehension: Pumas

The puma is a cat most recognized by the more popular names of "cougar" or "mountain lion." Just like other large cats, the puma is a carnivore. It feeds on deer, elk and other mammals. It can be found in both North and South America. Pumas have small heads with a single black spot above each eye. The coat color ranges from bluish-gray (North America) to reddish-brown (South America). The underside of the body, as well as the throat and muzzle, are white. The puma's body can be almost 6 feet long, not including the tail.

Female pumas give birth to two to four young. When first born, pumas have brown spots on their backs, and their tails are lined with dark brown rings.

As with the jaguar, pumas are blamed for killing cattle. Because of this, pumas are either nonexistent in some areas or are endangered.

Directions: Answer these questions about pumas.

1. What is a muzzle? *Answers will vary.*

2. As the population increases in North America, predict what might happen to pumas.
_____ *Answers will vary.*

3. What are two other popular names for the puma? cougar, mountain lion
4. What other cat besides the puma is blamed for killing cattle? jaguar
5. Reviewing the sizes of cats discussed so far, write their names in order, from smallest to largest.
1) lynx   2) puma
3) leopard   4) jaguar

90

Comprehension: Cheetahs

The cheetah can be found on the continent of Africa. Small numbers of cheetahs also live in Iran. Because its range has been drastically reduced, the cheetah is now endangered in tropical Africa. Because of its diminishing population and area, cheetahs are inbreeding, which affects genetic variations in the species. These variations can cause weaknesses to arise in the population.

The cheetah has a yellowish-brown coat with black spots. Cheetah's bodies grow to almost 5 feet long. Cheetahs are nearly the same weight as leopards, at about 130 pounds, but they have longer legs and bodies.

Unlike other cats, cheetahs are not capable of retracting their claws. They use their sense of sight rather than smell to hunt. The cheetah is the fastest animal on land. It can reach speeds of 68 miles per hour and, therefore, is able to outrun its prey.

Cheetahs often travel alone. Females only travel in groups when raising their cubs. Male cheetahs travel with females only during mating season.

Directions: Answer these questions about cheetahs.

1. What are the qualities that help a cheetah to hunt?
Cheetahs are very fast and have keen vision.

2. What is the danger to a species when inbreeding takes place?
weakness in the population

Directions: Use context clues for these definitions.

3. range: _____
4. diminishing: _____
5. genetic: _____ *Answers will vary.*
6. variations: _____

91

Comprehension: Tigers

Tigers live on the continent of Asia. The tiger is the largest cat, often weighing over 500 pounds. Its body can grow to be 9 feet long and the tail up to 36 inches in length.

There are three types of tigers. The Siberian tiger is very rare and has a yellow coat with dark stripes. The Bengal tiger can be found in southeastern Asian and central India. Its coat is more orange and its stripes are darker. There is a tiger that lives on the island of Sumatra as well. It is smaller and darker in color than the Bengal tiger.

Tigers lead solitary lives. They meet with other tigers only to mate and share food or water. Tigers feed primarily on deer and cattle but are also known to eat fish and frogs. If necessary, tigers will also eat dead animals.

Female tigers bear one to six cubs at a time. The cubs stay with their mother for almost 2 years before going out on their own.

Because tiger parts are in high demand for use in Chinese medicine and recipes, tigers have been hunted almost to extinction. All tigers are currently listed as endangered.

Directions: Use context clues for these definitions.

1. rare: _____
2. solitary: _____ *Answers will vary.*
3. extinction: _____

Directions: Answer these questions about tigers.

4. Why have tigers been hunted almost to extinction?
Their body parts are used in Chinese medicine and recipes.

5. Name the three types of tigers.
Siberian, Bengal and Sumatran

92

Comprehension: Lions

The lion, often referred to as the king of beasts, once commanded a large territory. Today, their territory is very limited. Lions are savanna-dwelling animals, which has made them easy targets for hunters. The increasing population of humans and their livestock has also contributed to the lion's decreased population.

Lions are heavy cats. Males weigh over 500 pounds and can grow to be over 8 feet in length, with a tail over 36 inches long. Males are characterized by a long, full mane that covers the neck and most of the head and shoulders. Females do not have a mane and are slightly smaller in size. Both males and females have beige coats, hooked claws and powerful jaws. Their roars can be heard up to 5 miles away!

Lions tend to hunt in the evening and spend the day sleeping. They prefer hunting zebra or giraffe but will eat almost anything. A lion is capable of eating over 75 pounds of meat at a single kill and then go a week without eating again. Generally, female lions do the hunting, and the males come to share the kill.

Lions live in groups called prides. Each pride has between 4 and 37 lions. Females bear one to four cubs approximately every 2 years.

Directions: Answer these questions about lions.

1. What are the differences between male and female lions? Male lions have a mane of hair and are larger in size.

2. Why would living on a savanna make the lion an "easy target"? _____

Directions: Use context clues for these definitions.

3. pride: _____ *Answers will vary.*
4. territory: _____
5. savanna: _____
6. capable: _____

93

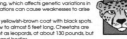

Recalling Details: Big Cats

Directions: Complete the chart with the information you learned about big cats. You may need reference books or the Internet to help you answer some of these questions.

Some answers will vary.

	Size	Color	# of Young	Food	Location
Jaguar	73 inches	yellowish-red with black spots	1 to 4	wide range of animals	Central and South America
Leopard	6 feet	light beige with black spots		monkeys, baboons, mice, fruit	Africa and Asia
Lynx	51 inches			small mammals and birds	U.S., Europe, Asia, Canada
Puma	6 feet	blueish-grey to redish-brown	2 to 4	deer, elk and other mammals	North and South America
Cheetah	5 feet	yellow-brown with black spots			Africa and Iran
Tiger	9 feet	yellow or orange with dark stripes	1 to 6	deer, cattle, fish and frogs	Asia
Lion	8 feet	golden beige	1 to 4	zebra and giraffe	savannas

94

Review

Directions: Follow the instructions below.

1. Choose any two big cats from this section and compare them.

2. Why is each of these big cats endangered or decreasing in number?

Answers will vary.

3. What can b_____ ____gered list?

4. Now that you have read about big cats, compare and contrast them with a house cat. What do you know now that you didn't know before reading this section?

95

Using Prior Knowledge: Famous Ships

Directions: Before reading about famous ships in the following section, answer these questions.

1. Look up the following terms in a dictionary and write their definitions.

vessel: _____
bow: _____
stern: _____
poop deck: _____
hull: _____
caravel: _____
mast: _____
frigate: _____
lateen: _____
spar: _____
fore: _____
aft: _____

Answers will vary.

2. Have you ever been on a large ship? If so, describe the experience. If not, on what kind of ship or boat would you like to ride? Why?

3. Name at least one famous ship and write what you know about it.

96

Comprehension: The *Constitution*

The *Constitution*, or "Old Ironsides," was built by the United States Navy in 1798. Its success in battle made it one of the most famous vessels in the United States. The Constitution's naval career began with the war with Tripoli from 1803 to 1804. Later, it was also used in the War of 1812. During this war, it was commanded by Isaac Hull. The *Constitution* won a 30-minute battle with the British ship, *Guerriere*, in August of 1812. The *Guerriere* was nearly demolished. Later that same year, the *Constitution* was used to capture a British frigate near Brazil.

The *Constitution* was taken out of service in 1829 and was rebuilt many times over the years. Today, it is on display at the Boston Navy Yard.

Directions: Answer these questions about the *Constitution*.

1. What is the main idea of t___ Answers will vary.

2. Which ship was almost demolished by the *Constitution*? _Guerriere_

3. In which two wars was the *Constitution* used? _war with Tripoli, War of 1812_

4. Where is the *Constitution* now on display? _Boston Navy Yard_

5. Complete the following time line with dates and events described above.

Constitution was built	War with Tripoli	War of 1812 Battle-*Guerriere*	Taken out of service	on display at Boston Navy Yard
1798	1803-1804	1812	1829	Today (1999)

97

Comprehension: The *Santa Maria, Niña and Pinta*

When Christopher Columbus decided to attempt a voyage across the ocean, the ships he depended upon to take him there were called "caravels." A caravel is a small sailing ship built by Spain and Portugal in the 15th and 16th centuries. The caravels Columbus used to sail to the New World were named Santa Maria, Niña, and Pinta.

The ships were not very large. It is believed the Santa Maria was only 75 to 90 feet long, and the Niña and Pinta were only about 70 feet long. Caravels typically had three to four masts with sails attached. The foremast carried a square sail, while the others were more triangular in shape. These triangular-shaped sails were called "lateen sails."

These three small ships were quite seaworthy and proved excellent ships for Columbus. They got him where he wanted to go.

Directions: Answer these questions about the *Santa Maria, Niña* and *Pinta*.

1. What is a lateen sail? _triangular-shaped_

2. What is the main idea of the selection? Answers will vary.

3. What is a caravel? _small sailing ships built by Portugal and Spain_

4. Where did Columbus sail in his caravels? _to the New World_

5. Do some research and compare a 15th-century caravel with a ship built in the 20th century.

Answers will vary.

98

Comprehension: The *Lusitania*

The *Lusitania* was a British passenger steamship. It became famous when it was torpedoed and sunk by the Germans during World War I. On May 7, 1915, the *Lusitania* was traveling off the coast of Ireland when a German submarine fired on it without warning. The ship stood no chance of surviving the attack and sank in an astonishing 20 minutes. 1,198 people perished, of whom 128 were American citizens. At the time the ship was torpedoed, the United States was not yet involved in the war. Public opinion over the attack put pressure on President Woodrow Wilson to declare war on Germany. The Germans proclaimed that the *Lusitania* was carrying weapons for the use of the allies.

This claim was later proven to be true. President Wilson demanded that the German government apologize for the sinking and make amends. Germany did not accept responsibility but did promise to avoid sinking any more passenger ships without first giving a warning.

Directions: Answer these questions about the *Lusitania*.

1. What does **proclaimed** mean? _____

2. What does **perished** mean? _____

3. What does _____

4. What does a_____ Answers will vary.

5. If the *Lusitania* was carrying arms, do you think the Germans had a right to sink it? Why or why not?

99

Page 100

Comprehension: The *Titanic*

The British passenger ship, *Titanic*, debuted in the spring of 1912. It was billed as an unsinkable ship due to its construction. It had 16 watertight compartments that would hold the ship afloat even in the event that four of the compartments were damaged.

But on the evening of April 14, 1912, during *Titanic's* first voyage, its design proved unworthy. Just before midnight, *Titanic* struck an iceberg, which punctured 5 of the 16 compartments. The ship sunk in a little under 3 hours.

Approximately 1,513 of the over 2,220 people onboard died. Most of these people died because there weren't enough lifeboats to accommodate everyone onboard. These people were left floating in the water. Many died from exposure, since the Atlantic Ocean was near freezing in temperature. It was one of the worst ocean disasters in history.

Because of the investigations that followed the *Titanic* disaster, the passenger ship industry instituted many reforms. It is now required that there is ample lifeboat space for all passengers and crew. An international ice patrol and full-time radio coverage were also instituted to prevent such disasters in the future.

Directions: Answer these questions about the *Titanic*.

1. How did most of the 1,513 people on board the *Titanic* die? **exposure to cold**

2. Why did this "unsinkable" ship sink? **an iceberg punctured too many of its compartments**

3. What changes have been made in ship safety as a result of the *Titanic* tragedy? **They must have enough lifeboats, international ice patrol, full-time radio coverage.**

4. There have been many attempts to rescue artifacts from the *Titanic*. But many families of the dead wish the site to be left alone, as it is the final resting place of their relatives. They feel burial sites should not be disrupted. Do you agree or disagree? Why?

Answers will vary.

100

Page 101

Venn Diagram: *Lusitania* and *Titanic*

A **Venn diagram** is used to chart information that shows similarities and differences between two things.

Example:

Dogs	Both	Cats
barks	good pet	one size
dependent	can live inside or outside	kills mice
large and small breeds	has fur	can use litterbox
protects the home	four legs	independent

Directions: Complete the Venn diagram for the *Lusitania* and the *Titanic*.

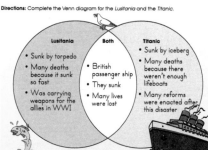

Lusitania
- Sunk by torpedo
- Many deaths because it sunk so fast
- Was carrying weapons for the allies in WWI

Both
- British passenger ship
- They sunk
- Many lives were lost

Titanic
- Sunk by iceberg
- Many deaths because there weren't enough lifeboats
- Many reforms were enacted after this disaster

101

Page 102

Comprehension: The *Monitor* and the *Virginia*

During the Civil War, it became customary to cover wooden warships with iron. This increased their durability and made them more difficult to sink. Two such ships were built using iron. They were the *Monitor* and the *Virginia*.

Most people are more familiar with the name the *Merrimack*. The *Merrimack* was a U.S. steam frigate that had been burnt and sunk by Union forces when the Confederates were forced to abandon their navy yard. The Confederate Navy raised the hull of the *Merrimack* and rebuilt her as the ironclad *Virginia*.

Both the *Monitor* and the *Virginia* engaged in battle on March 9, 1962. After several hours of battle, the bulky *Virginia* had no choice but to withdraw in order to avoid the lowering tides. This battle, called Hampton Roads, was considered to be a tie between the two ships.

Although both ships survived the battle, they were later destroyed. Two months later, the *Virginia* was sunk by her crew to avoid capture. The *Monitor* was sunk on December 31, 1862, during a storm off the coast of North Carolina.

Directions: Use context clues for these definitions.

1. customary: _____
2. durability: **Answers will vary.**
3. ironclad: _____

Directions: Answer these questions about the *Monitor* and the *Virginia*.

4. Who won the battle between the *Virginia* and the *Monitor*? **It was a tie.**

5. Why would lowering tides p_____ **Answers will vary.**

6. Describe how each ship was finally destroyed. **The *Virginia* was sunk by its crew to avoid capture. The *Monitor* was sunk in a storm.**

102

Page 103

Review

1. Use the Venn diagram you completed comparing the *Lusitania* and the *Titanic* (page 101) to write a two-paragraph compare/contrast essay about the two ships. Describe their similarities in the first paragraph and their differences in the second.

Answers will vary.

2. Describe the differences in the structure of the following ships: *Santa Maria, Monitor* and *Titanic*.
The *Santa Maria* was a relatively small sailing ship.
The *Monitor* was an iron-clad warship.
The *Titanic* was a luxury passenger ship built with 16 air-tight compartments to make it "unsinkable."

3. Why did people think the *Titanic* was unsinkable? After the ship actually did sink, how do you think this affected the way people thought about new technology?
The *Titanic* was constructed with 16 air-tight compartments.

Answers will vary.

103

Page 104

Cumulative Review

Directions: Follow the instructions below.

1. Write a paragraph comparing folk music and jazz music.

Answers will vary.

2. Complete the following chart with information from the section about farm animals.

	Pigs	Cows	Sheep	Goats
Gestation period (if known)	16 weeks	40 weeks	150 days	
Number of young for each pregnancy	10 to 14	1	1, 2 or 3	2 or 3
Human uses for this animal	meat bristles for brushes	meat milk leather	meat wool	milk
Interesting fact about the animal	Answers will vary.			

3. Write a description of each type of book.

legend: **a traditional story of myth**

nonfiction: **based on fact**

fiction: **non-factual literature**

104

Cumulative Review

4. Refer to the selection "Cooking With Care" (page 41). According to the author, what are the four main reasons people like to cook?

1) Home-cooked food tastes better.

2) It is a way of showing love.

3) The smell of home cooking has great appeal.

4) It brings the family together.

5. Give three examples of foods that...

Answers will vary.

1) _____ 3) _____

6. In the selection "The French Eat Differently" (page 45), the author discusses several differences between the French diet and the American diet. Write a paragraph discussing these differences.

Answers will vary.

7. What was the main responsibility of each god or goddess?

Jupiter _ruled all other gods_   Apollo _raised and lowered the sun_

Ceres _made things grow_   Venus _goddess of love and beauty_

8. What is the moral of the story of Apollo and Phaethon?

Answers will vary.

9. According to the story of Proserpine, Pluto and Ceres, what occurs on a regular basis due to the agreement between Pluto and Jupiter?

the changing of seasons

105

Cumulative Review

10. List at least one major accomplishment of each of the following artists.

Leonardo da Vinci _____

Michelangelo _____ Answers will vary.

Rembrandt _____

11. What does it mean to "counterfeit" a stamp?

Make a fake that looks nearly identical to the original.

12. List at least one fact about each of the following ships.

Titanic _____

Lusitania _____

Virginia _____ Answers will vary.

Monitor _____

Constitution _____

13. Write three reasons why many big cats are endangered today.

1) _____

2) _____ Answers will vary.

3) _____

14. Why is it important to "study the market" before trying to have a piece of writing published?

Carefully read a copy of a magazine you would like to be published in.

15. What are the names of three magazines that publish children's writing?

1) _____

2) _____ Answers will vary.

3) _____

106

Teaching Suggestions

Comprehension

As you read with your child, encourage him/her to picture in his/her mind what is happening. This will help your child recall the story using the "mind's eye," as well as the ear. Ask him/her to retell the story, noting details from the beginning, middle and end.

Your child is now reading "chapter books." These books usually have very few pictures. Check your child's comprehension by having him/her draw pictures representing the action or the problem for each chapter. Before starting each new chapter, ask your child to predict what will happen.

Invite your child to write a different ending or new chapter to a story. If your child can do this in a logical manner, he/she has grasped the plot or ideas presented.

Following Directions

Invite your child to put together a model or read about how to play a new game, following the directions. Point out the importance of clear, easy-to-understand directions, as well as following them in the correct order.

To reinforce this concept, prepare a recipe with your child. Ask him/her what would happen if you skipped a step, completed the steps out of order or left out an ingredient. Your child will realize the importance of writing and following specific directions.

Main Idea

Invite your child to group things into categories to see if the concept, or main idea, is understood. Examples: wild animals, sports played outside, board games, books about American women.

Show your child that in his/her textbooks, such as science, the chapters or units are grouped according to the main idea: The Human Body, Space, and so on.

Ask your child questions while reading together, such as, "What is the most important thing the author is saying in this paragraph?" "Can you tell what the author is saying in one sentence?"

Recalling Details

Write ideas on index cards, such as **summer vacation**. Then ask your child to write several details about the idea, such as **no school, playing with friends, camping, riding bikes**, and so on.

Write a simple sentence for your child. Example: **The cat ran down the street**. Show your child how adding details makes the sentence more interesting. Example: **The fluffy white cat ran quickly down the noisy street**. Ask him/her to add details to several simple sentences. Point out that these kinds of details are usually describing words, or adjectives.

Take this idea one step further and have your child write a story about a family trip or a day at the mall, the beach or a friend's party. Encourage him/her to include lots of details about what happened.

Word Origins

Help your child research your family name and your family tree. When did your ancestors arrive in America? How did they arrive? Have any changes been made to the spelling of your surname?

Invite your child to find words that originate from Native American words. The states of Florida, Ohio and New Jersey have many towns and lakes named by Native Americans. Ask your child to trace the names to a specific tribe.

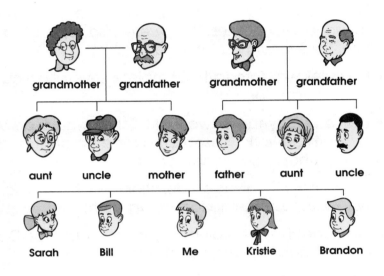

Guide your child to see that, although Latin is not a spoken language, many of the words in the English language are derived from Latin words. For example, the words **amiable**, **fictitious**, **liquid**, **major**, **omit** and **poet** all have Latin origins. Invite your child to trace these and other words to the Latin words from which they derived.

Writing

To review the topics in this book more in-depth, invite your child to write short essays or journal entries on some of the following topics. Encourage him/her to write complete sentences and include lots of details supporting his/her ideas.

- Write an opinion essay about whether or not animals should be placed in zoos.

- The *Hindenburg* was a blimp involved in a major air disaster. Compare and contrast this tragedy with the *Titanic*.

- What is the best fictional book you have read? Why do you like it?

Hindenburg vs. Titanic

- Choose a song you particularly enjoy. What qualities does it have? Do the words hold special meaning for you? Why?

- Vegetarians do not eat meat. Does your family eat meat? If so, why? If not, why not?

- People who live in the country have the benefit of being around both wild and domestic animals. People who live in the city have pets, but do not regularly have the opportunity to see cows, sheep, pigs, and so on. What are the advantages and disadvantages of both city and country living? If you had a choice, which would you prefer? Why?

- During the 1940s, many Jewish people, like Esther Hautzig (see page 33), were forced to leave their homes. They were also separated from family and friends. Describe the emotions they must have felt.

- Hercules was forced to complete several difficult tasks. Research these tasks and write a paragraph on each.

- Do you enjoy the artwork of Michelangelo, da Vinci and Rembrandt? Or do you prefer modern artwork? Research a modern artist and compare/contrast his/her work with one of those mentioned above.

- Research the salvage operations on the *Titanic*. Discuss some of the major findings and who was responsible for finding them.

- Machines have a valuable place in our lives. Discuss one machine that you could not live without. Explain your answer.

- Each year, the United States Postal Service looks for new stamp designs. Think of a stamp design or a person you believe should appear on a stamp. Explain why you think this stamp is important, and then draw the design on a separate sheet of paper. Remember, a person appearing on a stamp can no longer be living.